Warrior Wives

A Collection of Stories from the Wives, Girlfriends and
Children of The Royal Marines and The Royal Navy.

By

Elizabeth Eager

Foreword by

Chris Terrill

The stories and illustrations in this book have been provided with permission given to the author for sharing. Some of the names have been changed to protect identities of those still serving.

The illustrations were provided with thanks from Goosewell Primary School.

Produced in collaboration with The Royal Navy and Royal Marines Children's Fund.

Design and layout:
Tim Mitchell Design
www.tim-mitchell.co.uk

For Adele, and my 'Band of Wives' (Abandoned wives),
And for my husband.

- Your strength taught me to be Strong.

Warrior Wives

Wives And Girlfriends
Deserve Medals Too

When a Royal Marine Commando deploys to the front line with all its lethal risks to life and limb he does not do so alone. He is with his comrades of course, his brothers in arms who he would die for, but he is with others too, at least in spirit: the women in his life who he lives and breathes for. These may be a girlfriend, a wife, a mother or a daughter – the loved ones he has left behind and who will be longing for his return and praying for his safety. They may be far away in distance, in physical miles, but in other ways they could not be closer for they will be in his heart and in his mind. The memory of them, their imagined faces, their soft embrace, their ringing voices and echoing laughter, will at once sadden him but empower him and strengthen his resolve. Reinforced by the fortifying knowledge of this love and devotion at home, the warrior marches on – his duty to perform.

The same is true of the sailor who ventures out on to the high seas in defence of his nation. He will have waved tearful goodbyes to his nearest and dearest standing on the Round Tower in Pompey or Devil's Point in Guzz as his ship of war heads for the South Atlantic or somewhere east of Suez. That sailor, like the marine, will be bolstered by the thought of those he is leaving behind and who he knows will be on the quayside when his ship returns.

This remarkable book tells the story of those left behind – not the warriors or seafarers but the womenfolk who in many ways have the tougher mission to perform and more exacting deployment to endure as they wait and pray for that safe return when the family will once again be complete. But there's the rub. Supposing there is no safe return; supposing disaster strikes and tragedy ensues.

This was the case for the thirteen long years of the war in Afghanistan of course when the constant fear of injury or death to their men haunted girlfriends, wives, mothers, sisters and daughters every hour of every day they were away.

A soldier or sailor trains for war, prepares for risk and braces for danger. They are helped to become 'battle-ready' but not so a wife or girlfriend.

How does she train for enforced solitude; gear up for tension and trepidation every time she switches on the news or, worst of all, practice for that terrifying knock on the door?

Being a military wife or girlfriend demands a special sort of courage, a very distinct sort of valour and a remarkable brand of selflessness and loyalty. A good friend of mine, a Royal Marine Commando awarded the Military Cross in Afghanistan but badly injured by an IED, still maintains that his wife endured more than he did.

"We don't understand what they have to put up with" he confided in me. "It's not just the loneliness and having to look after the kids on their own. It's the constant fear of being told we have been killed or injured. And if injured, as in my case, it was then having to be strong for both of us when I got home. My wife was there for me not only when I was physically weak but also when I was in a mess from the night terrors and flashbacks from combat. My mate saved me on the front line by stemming my blood flow but my wife saved me at home by being my constant strength and hope. Oh yes – she deserves a medal and no mistake".

Military wives and girlfriends are the unsung heroes of any war, of any deployment, of any mission. Read this book and understand military service from a different point of view. Prepare to laugh, prepare to cry but above all prepare to be moved, inspired and uplifted.

Chris Terrill

Introduction

So, why did I choose to write this book?

It started as a small, niggling idea a few years ago. My husband and I had recently been reunited after a four month long separation and were attending the wedding of a civilian friend. It was the first time I had been to a non-military wedding in a while. Certainly the first one I'd been too with my husband by my side as he is too often away for celebrations. We had family available as babysitters and were excited to have a rare night off, together. We were sat at the bar, chatting together and catching up on the last four months and we started talking to some other wedding guests. It emerged in conversation that my husband was serving in the Royal Marines and had recently been away. My husband is not someone who likes to be centre of attention but he is still fond of telling people about his travels – "spinning dits" as it is called in the Royal Marines. From the outset my contribution to the conversation was minimal, and I felt this insignificance and invisibility increase as the conversation turned to his deployment in Afghanistan, and previously Iraq. As my husband fielded questions from the ridiculous "So, have you actually held a gun? A real one?" to the politically difficult "Do you think you've made a difference in Afghanistan? Should we be there? Or are we making it worse?" to the personal "Do you find it hard being away from your son?" No one even considered asking how my son and I felt being away from him.

I sipped my drink and smiled with pride should anyone actually make eye contact with me. Because, I am incredibly proud of my husband's career; I always have been.

But I also started to feel a little jealous; envious of the ever growing crowd of interested people that were distracting my husband's attention. We had not had a single night out together in nearly a year, and had been apart completely for four months up until a few days before this wedding – I didn't want to share his attention! I nursed my solitary glass of wine and watched as my husband got bought beer after beer. No one asked how Afghanistan was for me.

It started me thinking of all the wives who, like me, are quietly conditioned to let our husbands shine; to smile with pride, whilst swallowing down the jealousy his career creates. Not jealous because I don't trust him, or because I would consider myself a worthy opponent of the Taleban. I am not a hero. I am not brave, not in the way that he is brave. But jealous of the adventures he has had, the places he gets to travel to, the history he is a part of making, the stories he has to tell. Ultimately, jealous of the time he is taken away from me. The memories he gets to make without me being part of them; the part of his life that I cannot share.

I understand that their stories are full of more bravery and fraught with more excitement and danger, and I'd like to be very clear that I do not consider myself even half as brave as any service man, or woman, who defends our country. They command my upmost respect.

The only explosions you may find in these pages are of nappies, or tears.

The only 'near misses' are the phone calls we frantically search in our handbags for, pulling onto the side of the road, or standing in the middle of the supermarket, or playground to speak with our husbands or lovers for twenty or thirty, precious few, minutes a week.

The only stand out acts of bravery are not pulling our wounded comrade from the battlefield, but tucking our children into bed with kisses, wiping their tears and promising that Daddy will be home soon; or just lending a listening ear to a friend in need when we feel equally needy. Just getting dressed, going to work and surviving each day living with a heart that feels broken and empty for days, weeks, or even months on end.

We often spend our marriages counting down until the day he leaves the military and can really be 'ours', and we face the transition from military to civilian life, with trepidation, fear and excitement; often signposting the way for our husbands, because we have walked the line between military life and civilian life for years. Our stories may not be great adventure stories, we may not risk life and limb, but we are prepared to face the consequences when our husbands do and we alter our 'happily ever after' for so many different reasons.

These are not Heroes stories, they are Lover's stories.

They may not be exciting or thrilling, but they are tales of strength, independence and quiet courage and patience. And ultimately tales of Love; our Love stories are our legacy.

We may not deserve medals, but our stories deserve to be told, read or listened to, and maybe, just maybe, we deserve to be bought a beer once in a while too....

Taylor 10

" When my Daddy's away I be the man of the house and have extra hugs with Mummy."

Tyler-Lee, 6

It Runs in the Family

Emma, Royal Marine Daughter and Girlfriend

I grew up with the Royal Marines and they were my idols. My Dad was, and still is, my hero.

I am so proud to tell anyone and everyone that my Dad was a Royal Marine! Alongside my parents, my Dad's 'lads' played a big part in bringing me up for the first couple of years of my life. My Mum battled with some health issues and a back injury, so whilst we lived in Northern Ireland my Godfather, Dominic or 'Salty' as he was known, and my Dad took turns looking after me in between daily patrols and duty.

Growing up, I missed my Dad every time he went away, but Mum always found ways to ensure we didn't miss out on anything and she took on the role of both Mum and Dad while he was away.

I guess I really remember the times spent together as a family more than the time spent apart; because my parents ensured we spent quality time together every chance we had. Being in a military family, you know that time is so precious and we took advantage of every minute.

We 'lived on the patch'[1] and we were surrounded by support and friends. As kids it was great fun and felt like one big family. It is not until now that I truly realise how incredible and strong my Mum is. I often went through phases of feeling annoyed with my Mum as it was her who had to say 'no' or ground us. Now I realise that in order to juggle work, two kids and a dog she had to be strict, independent and ensure her rules were respected and followed, because my Dad was not always there to back her up. My Dad eventually learnt to slot back into our lives without un-settling our routine too much.

We were sheltered from the harsh reality of the risks that came with Dads' job.

He rarely told us of his deployment experiences but I can appreciate that what he has been through may not be something he would want to share with his children.

I remember being woken up once in the early hours of the morning to my Dad passing us black clothes and face 'cam-cream' (camouflage cream). His lads were on an island in the bay behind our house doing a military

---

1. a 'Married Patch' refers to a military housing estate.

exercise[2]. He suspected they were 'not quite taking the task seriously', so he rowed out with us in the dingy and had us act out the motions of laying an IED[3] at the base of the bridge with some wire. We thought this was awesome! The lads did eventually end up radioing the sighting and 'intel' in, but they were confused as to how to describe the small humans spotted; I assume due to a low expectation of seeing two children disguised as enemy in the middle of the night.

I was the wrong sex to join the Royal Marine's, so I joined the Army Reserves as a Combat Medic. It was whilst working away, and being attached with the Royal Marines that I met my other half Kris.

My Dad caught wind of our dating and asked me for detailed information on Kris, and he may have spoken to a few old 'oppo's' still in the Corps to be sure Kris was a good lad. Two years later and we are still happy so he must have passed the checks.

I think having experience growing up with the military had its advantages and disadvantages; I knew what to expect with Kris being away, and had already mastered coping strategies, but again I knew what to expect. The separation, the worry, the unknown, not being able to set plans, the possibility of injury or illness...

I think no matter how busy you make yourself, how much support you have around you or how many coping strategies you have, sometimes nothing can help that sinking feeling of missing him. But - as we all do, we just get on with it. Then he gets home and with that feeling of being held tight in his arms all the pain of missing him is gone. Until next time. I recently completed the thirty mile Commando Survival Yomp[4] carrying full Commando weight. It was tough to say the least! My Dad and Brother came to support me and met me at the twenty five mile mark at the Commando Memorial. We laid a photo and pin down for my God father 'Salty' who had cared for me a lot when I was very young. He had unfortunately been killed during a training exercise with the Marines, years before.

I have never felt so emotional; I told Salty that 'I had walked twenty five miles to do this and I hoped I was making him proud'. I cannot

---

2. 'Exercise' is the military term given to a practise of standard war time procedures.
3. An IED is improvised explosive device/bomb.
4. Yomp is another term for Walk/Hike.

describe how hard it is to see the hurt and sadness my Dad still feels today, over the loss of his comrade, his 'Brother'. My Dad is the strongest man I know and sometimes I find it hard to stomach the thought that being in a relationship with a Marine now, I may have to go through watching such loss all over again and sharing his grief. Maybe I am being melodramatic but loss is hard to deal with and is unfortunately, inevitable when connected to the military.

Kris has been completely accepted as part of our family; so much so that my Mum calls him son. My poor Mum thought she had done her time being the strong one while my Dad was away but now she is experiencing it from a different perspective and with my Brother joining up next year it looks like we will always be a Royal Marine family.

"Daddy trains people to fight and he goes away a lot."

Abbie, 7

Half Woman, Half Machine

Shelley, Royal Marine Wife

So, when you marry a Marine, not only do you sign up for a life of extreme highs and extreme lows, you soon come to realise that you have to share your life. Not only with your husband, but also with the other 6000 odd men that make up the Royal Marine Corps.

This can be a very difficult thing to get your head around to start with. I feel that people outside the military world will never truly know what we as wives have to go through. Sometimes, people take for granted what they have in the way of support. In our world we don't always have that luxury, quite often our husbands may not be at the birth of our children, they may miss all the scans and the excitement that goes along with expecting a child. Little things like having your husband home every night, being there when you or your children are poorly, are all missed. The special milestones you so desperately want to share with them, all missed.

Our lives can be so lonely and hard but, when they are home all the hardships are soon forgotten and the roller coaster ride of happiness and joy begins, this coupled with the immense pride we feel for our husbands soon makes any troubles seem like a far distant memory.

Here is a little about me and my world; I met my husband in a well known watering hole in Exeter, and from that moment I fell in love. I spent the next month or so trying to pursue him hoping, by some strange twist of fate, that we would meet again. I'm happy to say that we did and since then, have never looked back. At the time we first met he was in training to be a Royal Marine Commando. I supported him though training and watched with pride when he passed out in the summer of 2008. Two months later the news, that I and every other wife or girlfriend dreads, came; he was off to Afghanistan.

He left two weeks before Christmas and waiting for that day to come was hell. I lay in bed with him asleep in my arms, usually snoring and dribbling, but treasuring every second worrying that this could be the last time I got to do this. So the day arrived that he had to leave, and I will never forget it. I stood outside Bickleigh barracks and waved goodbye. Holding back the tears I can remember praying in my head saying over and over again like a mantra: "please bring this man home to me, please bring this man home to me".

15

The front of the camp was full of flowers and tributes for the fallen soldiers that we had already lost, and this almost tipped me over the edge. As he walked away, I burst out in a flood of tears.

As a military wife there is one thing you do not want to hear whilst they are deployed, and that is "Stop worrying! He will be ok" and that is all anyone seemed to tell me. I guess some people actually have no idea what these men and their wives go through!

It was the longest six months of my life, with poor communication. The worry was crippling, sitting by the phone never wanting to miss a phone call, because as morbid as it sounds it could be the last time you get to speak to him. Or because you know how desperately they need to hear about home; not just want to, but actually need to be reminded of normality.

He returned two days after my birthday. He hadn't even told me when he was coming back. I just had a knock at the door and he was standing there! I threw my arms around him and that's where they stayed for the next four weeks. We decided to get married and start trying for a baby. Now in the normal world, trying for a baby is easy. However this proves difficult having a partner in the forces as they are never home to make the baby at the right times! After nine months of trying and a few medical problems, I did what felt like the hundredth pregnancy test in nine months expecting that same negative result when two lines appeared. It was positive! We were overjoyed! I had to go to the scans alone which can seem very unfair but I got used to it. We married while I was pregnant and moved into our first house on a patch and five weeks later we had our first baby boy. I was meant to be home on my own that week but luckily my husband didn't need to go away. Needless to say it can be tough and lonely when it was just me and our little man home alone, and not having anyone to share the load. You are kind of Mum and Dad in one body and have to give your children everything they need, reassure them Daddy isn't away because he wants to be and that he misses them too.

Two years later and after three failed pregnancies I was pregnant again. But the labour was quick, so quick in fact that he was very nearly born on the way to hospital. My husband's face was pure panic as I said "I think I need to push!" It still makes me giggle now and I am so grateful he was there to share it with me, I know other wives who aren't so lucky.

Now I think my children sometimes think their Daddy is a bit of a superhero; Action Man, or as my Son says, Danger Mouse. I have no idea what my boys think happens on a daily basis in my husband's work but they think he has his own tank, lots of guns and is always fighting bad guys, oh and flying - flying lots of helicopters!

We have always been really honest with our children and the routine is always the same whether my husband is home or not. It has to be, to keep me sane. But it can be heartbreaking when they say "Why is my Daddy not here?" and "other peoples Daddies never have to go away". My answer is always the same: "Daddy is helping people and has to go away, aren't you lucky to have such a brave Daddy!" I try to make it a positive thing rather than them missing out.

Our house is happy and full of laughter and fun. We are a happy family and even if I am finding things hard I would never let my children see that. People in the normal world have said to me "Why are you moaning? You knew what you were getting yourself into." No one ever knows before they marry a Marine how hard it is actually going to be; and I truly believe the men never know how hard it's going to be to keep saying goodbye to their families.

On a daily basis we face things other people will never have to and our children have to grow up very fast going through things and emotions most adults will never experience. But I wouldn't change the way we live. It can be bonkers and hard but it's so worth it. I've learnt so much about myself and what I can cope with. I've realised I am half woman, half highly tuned machine, that just seems to adapt and change plans, with a smile on my face.

Jaden, 8

"I play Lego with Mummy to stop me missing Daddy.

Austin, 4

Follow your Heart

Kirsty, Royal Marine Girlfriend (now wife!)

I first met Todd at a friend's barbecue at home in New Zealand. We started talking and found out that we both had one way tickets to London. Todd was going to pursue his life's dream of becoming a Royal Marine Commando, as his father and Grandfather had been. My plan was to have the traditional 'overseas adventure' - work and travel then come back home to New Zealand and continue working in the family business. Todd invited me on another date to a rock concert in a city three hours away, I instantly said yes. When he arrived to pick me up on a Harley Davidson, it was my Dad and Brother's worst nightmare - their baby girl getting picked up for a rock concert by a tattooed biker who wanted to join the military! After that concert, we spent every weekend together until Todd was due to fly out to the U.K. We said we would see how we could make it work out with him going into the Marines and me wanting to travel.

When I flew out we met in London. Whilst Todd was going through the process of joining - the exams, medicals, and PRMC[5] (pre training fitness test), we lived in a small village north of Newcastle. We worked together, lived together, did everything together. So, when Todd finally got his letter to say he would go into basic training on 11th February, I was devastated.

I looked for work near Exmouth and got a live in Au-pair job a short drive from Lympstone. I was lucky with my host family as they let Todd come and stay on the odd weekend he got off, and gave me time off to spend his Easter and summer leave with him.

During basic training it was so hard. I constantly battled with anxiety and mild depression as I was scared of being away from my family and Todd. I started to carry my phone with me twenty four hours a day - even into the bathroom while I showered. I would drop everything if I got a phone call or text. I would count down every week and make notes of how well Todd was going through training. When he passed out[6] in

---

5. PRMC is a four day intensive pre – training fitness test. Recruits have to pass this to be accepted onto training for the Royal Marines.
6. Pass out is the term given when they pass their training and are awarded the Green Beret.

October, his Mum, Dad, Nan and some friends flew over from New Zealand. We had a big party but it was also hard for me to share Todd with his family – I had missed him and just wanted him all to myself.

We decided I would go back to New Zealand until Todd was settled in his unit and so I could meet my new Niece and Nephew. I would also work the summer in New Zealand for my family.

I found that to be the hardest thing I have ever done, leaving Todd in the UK to pursue such a dangerous career and not knowing when I would see him again.

But we were lucky and Todd was granted Christmas leave so I got him a ticket home to New Zealand. But the Christmas reunion was stressful because we stayed with family, when really we just wanted to have our own personal space, to spend time together.

When Todd went back to the UK we thought he would get Easter leave and we planned to meet each other halfway perhaps in Thailand, but he didn't get leave. So, from Christmas until July we only had Skype and Viber - I am so grateful for modern technology! Some weeks we could Skype up to three times, or we could go three weeks at a time with only a couple of Viber messages; it was never constant or reliable. I kept busy with aerobics, running, I started pole and rock n' roll dancing! I didn't give myself a spare minute to stop and think of how much I was missing my best friend and lover. So after seven months apart Todd was finally coming home for his summer leave.

I went to the city to pick him up from the airport. When I saw him through the arrival gate in his uniform I couldn't help myself, I ran and jumped into his arms. We kissed and hugged and I cried and the crowd started clapping. He said he had a present that he needed to give me and then he got down onto one knee and asked me to marry him! He had the most gorgeous ring and I was overwhelmed with love and excitement. His brother and girlfriend were at the airport hiding from me the entire time and they filmed the proposal.

On the nights when I am lonely I watch it.

We made the decision to have special "us time" during this leave. We took off to stay in Hotels and we both loved every minute of it. We are now in the process of planning our elopement to Las Vegas for Christmas leave this year. It will just be the two of us. I am a real family girl and never thought I would elope. But I think this is going to be the most romantic time for just Todd and I, so special and intimate; just us two and not a wedding for everyone else. We will of course have a big party in New Zealand where we will have a first dance, cutting of a cake and speeches, but this will need to wait until Todd can come home again.

Getting married to Todd doesn't just mean I will be bonded with my best friend forever, but it also means I will need to leave my family and friends in my home country and move back to the UK to live, wherever Todd may be based. I am nervous for the future as I want to have a family but I want our children to know their cousins and grandparents, their family. I worry everyday because I will move back to the UK, but when Todd is deployed overseas, I will be left alone in the UK away from everyone I love and care about.

Then there is the fact Todd is going to be in the most dangerous situations throughout the world. I want to grow old and watch our grandchildren grow up - this is a fear and reality we just have to learn to live with everyday.

For me the hardest thing, to adjust to, was seeing the change in Todd from the innocent young guy I met, into a very life experienced man. I struggle with the fact I am not there for him every night and don't know everything he is going through - he tells me what he can but I know it's nothing to what is actually happening in his life.

I am so proud of my Marine, I wouldn't change him for the world. But, all I want is for him to be safe and happy. I have the support and love from both our families and I am lucky for that. However, nobody really understands how hard it really is or what we actually go through, but I do know our love is the strongest I could have ever dreamed of.

"Royal Marines protect the planet."

Matthew, 5.

21

One way Conversations
Jenny, Royal Marine Girlfriend.

If you'd have asked me three months ago, I would have said my toughest battle was our first full tour of Afghanistan. It was seven months of anxiety, worry, loneliness and separation. However, I am quickly learning that being with someone in the military is an ongoing series of challenges, not just when they are deployed.

We have just bought our first home, which should normally be a time of celebration and new beginnings. But not exactly for us! We only managed to pick up the keys, days before he went back to work, and he's hardly been here since. It's been left to me to sort out 'our' bills, unpack 'our' belongings and try to make it 'our' home; all by myself.

It's the first time I've ever lived by myself. Totally alone, getting used to creepy noises and double locking the door; having no one to talk to for days on end. Trying to look after the garden, the cellar and eating meals alone, not being able to contact him, not even just call him for some support whenever I want.

Sometimes, I get so lonely I find myself talking to the insects and spiders, just to fill the house with some sort of conversation; trying to fill up the void and the emptiness; all the time feeling painfully alone.

Now that I don't have my family around me either; I've realised what feeling lonely really is, which is ridiculous because I'm in a relationship.

My highest reward was my graduation. I received a first of which I am so incredibly proud. My partner wasn't there for the graduation ceremony, as he had to work; which tends to be the story of our life.

If I could give my past self advice it would be this; learn how to make friends wherever you are, so you never have to feel alone. Friendship is so important, especially in the life that we live.

I think once you've been in the military, or had a loved one join; it changes your outlook on life permanently. It's not just a job. It's an entire lifestyle – one, that is hard to live, but it's even harder to let go of.

Evie Mae.

"I write in my diary and count down the Days."

Abbie, 7

Not a Game of Soldiers

Rachael, Royal Marine Girlfriend.

Me and Kev, met online, ten years ago. I was really attracted to him but was actually totally put off by him being a Marine. He was hot, but I knew it wasn't the lifestyle for me. I had a baby with my previous partner and didn't want another serious relationship yet. So Kev and I had on and off contact but he still wanted something more and I just wasn't ready to commit to his lifestyle. I told Kev this and broke it off. One day after he'd been on a drunken night out, I woke up to eighty or more missed calls! I cut ties completely then, thinking "Jesus he's a stalker psycho". He tried to pull the 'Afghan card' by telling me he was going to deploy to get me to see him again before he left, but I still just wasn't ready for that.

Two years later I came across his name in my phone and I thought "I wonder what he's up to" and text him. He knew who it was straight away and we began speaking again but he was going back to Afghanistan again soon. This time I was ready. Our relationship started and I sent him parcels every week.

Afghan was hard; I didn't sleep or eat much, but because it was a new relationship, I didn't feel I fully had the right to worry as much as I did. He came back safely from Afghanistan and our relationship went from strength to strength.

However, another tough battle for me was when I fell pregnant and we found out Kev was going away on a training course over my due date. He didn't need to go but he wanted to and it would be good for his career. I didn't want him to go as I didn't want to go through labour alone but I couldn't tell him not to. That had to be his choice and he decided to go. I was heartbroken but I couldn't say that to him; I know how important his career is to him. As it happened, I had a premature baby that came seven weeks early so he didn't miss it after all. It was difficult but he decided not to do the course, or be away straight after baby Ollie was born. He stayed to help.

Being with the man of my dreams and having my amazing family is the only reward I need for me. Even though it's hard having him go away, it is worth it when he comes back.

We often have a blazing argument before he goes away, partly because I feel the need to push him away to make it easier for me, but I start missing him about four hours after he leaves. I have the kids for company but it's still lonely without him. I miss the little things. He acts like a macho man but he's one of the gentlest men I know.

Life in the military is tough. It's hard, and it isn't playing soldiers. If the things you see effect you, you should always look for help, it is not a weakness, it's just being human.

I think it's harder for the kids.

We have bought lots of books to help them cope, including ones about military families. Jack, my eldest, misses Kev immensely when he is away. One time Kev was only going on a training exercise and Jack turned around and said "I don't want you to go...I don't want you to die." This broke my heart hearing someone so innocent say something so powerful.

Kev is based where I am from and if he was drafted down south I'd be torn. Can I turn my kids' life upside down? Move away from school? Family? Friends? Everything they know? But on the other hand I couldn't bear to rip my family apart. When the time comes that will be the hardest decision I will ever make.

Being married to or in love with someone in the military is really hard, but love isn't meant to be easy. It is tough and frightening, and it pushes your relationship to the limits. But if it's true love you can be strong enough. You will have an amazing life and a future with the man of your dreams.

" I cuddle my cushion with Daddy's picture on "

Jason, 5

Turning 'Rock Bottom', into 'Top of the World.'

Becky Ormrod, Royal Marine Wife

I first met Mark when I moved to Plymouth to complete my top up degree at University. Mark had already left the Marines and was working as a bouncer in a very cheesy night club that I happened to love and go to at least twice a week. He would always talk to me and let me in for free and after a while he started pestering me for my number, but I played hard to get. It wasn't until after about a month of pestering that he decided to change tactics and say he would ban me if I didn't give him my number. I finally gave in out of fear of not being allowed back into my favourite club... the fact that I also thought he was incredibly hot helped, but I wasn't going to admit that. We went on a few dates and became inseparable. We fell in love very quickly and everything felt so right. We were just perfect together. However, Mark missed being in the Marines and after a lot of thought he decided to rejoin. That was in May and by the September he was deployed on Op Herrick 7 to Afghanistan. How did I feel about this? Well, Mark was doing something that I knew he absolutely loved and because I knew how happy being in the Marines made him, I supported him whole heartedly. It was his decision and he had to do what would make him happy.

After he left, as I think all wives or girlfriends do, I found myself watching the news all the time, but I had it in my head that nothing would happen to him. I just kept myself busy to help the time pass more quickly.

We sent each other blueys[7] all the time and Mark would call as much as possible, so we had really good contact, which made it easier. Then the count-down was on until Mark would be home on R and R - two weeks rest & relaxation at home.

I couldn't wait to see him. He was due home on the 29th December and he had already told me that guys were getting flown back to Camp Bastion from their FOB[8], (the base where they are stationed in between patrols) about a week before their R and R dates. So, I was expecting him to be safe already, and when I got a call on Christmas Eve to say that Mark had been

---

7. Blueys are the military nickname for letters
8. FOB stands for forward operating base, where they are based between patrols.

involved in an incident I was in total disbelief.

I was initially told he had lost a leg and it wasn't until later in the evening I found out that it was, in fact, both legs and his arm. I was in total denial. I honestly thought that they had got it wrong, and that it was someone else who was injured and not Mark. I didn't sleep at all that night and just lay in bed in complete shock, unable to stop crying.

It was on Christmas Day that my Dad took me to Selly Oak Hospital in Birmingham where Mark was getting flown into. Still thinking it couldn't possibly be him, I walked into ICU expecting to give a sigh of relief. But the first thing that I noticed was the smell! It was indescribable; the smell of open wounds, blood and dirt that had been cooked in the Afghan heat for some twenty plus hours. It is something I will, unfortunately never be able to forget; no matter how much I wish I could. The next thing I noticed was that it was him; it was my Mark lying there. He looked as if he was just sleeping, and in need of a shower. He didn't have a single scratch on his face and, whilst the smell still bothered me I didn't take any notice of the tubes coming out of him. I could actually ignore the flatness of the sheets where his feet should have been and the first thing I thought was that he's still gorgeous. He was still my Mark

Then it hit me: the emotions of seeing the man I love lying helplessly in front of me, not really knowing the extent of his injuries, or if he would even make it through, or how he would react if he did; I had to sit down before I fell down.

The next few days were a blur until the day Mark woke up: Incredibly weak, and still with an oxygen mask to help him breathe, Mark opened his eyes and started to say something. It was a mumble, and no matter how hard I tried I just couldn't understand what he was saying. He repeated it about eight times before I finally got it. The first thing my boyfriend asked upon waking was "Will you marry me?" Of course I didn't even hesitate and said yes!

Mark had planned to ask me the big question whilst on R and R, and he had even written a letter to my Dad asking for his permission.

I barely left Mark's side for the whole six weeks that he was in hospital. I would be there from the moment he woke up in the morning until he fell asleep at night. In general his morale was good and he was forever cracking jokes. But if you know any Marines, you know that is what they do; they laugh, and his Bootneck ethos really shone through. But there were dark days as well. The "top prosthetic guy" came to see Mark about three weeks after he was injured and told him that he would never walk again. He would be wheelchair bound and would manage two hours maximum on prosthetics. In a matter of minutes Mark went from having a positive outlook and being hopeful, to being completely broken and it was that evening that he broke his heart to me.

We both lay next to each other, tears streaming down our faces with Mark saying he couldn't cope. He couldn't do it and he didn't want to do it. He didn't want to be a burden on me or on anyone for that matter; he didn't want his daughter having to grow up with a cripple for a Dad, and he didn't want to live a life where he couldn't do all the things he loved. He asked me to help him end it all. That was the most heartbreaking conversation that we have ever had.

That night, I made Mark a promise: I would never give up on him, as long as he didn't give up on himself. We had hit rock bottom but I promised him things would get better. At the time I didn't know if things would get better but I believed in him. I knew he always gave 100% to everything he's ever done and that failure just wasn't an option, and I certainly wasn't going to let failure be an option now!

That was seven years ago and what a ride we have been on since. We have had our fair share of bad times but the good outweighs them by miles and everything that happens just makes us stronger!

We are now married and blessed with very beautiful children; Mason who is three and Evelyn who is eighteen months and of course Mark's daughter Kezia who is now ten.

Mark is no longer a serving Royal Marine so he will never go on deployment again; but he is still away a lot, and it's harder now than it was for me in 2007 because we've got the kids. As they've got older they notice more when Daddy's not here and they miss him so much. Technology and FaceTime is a blessing as they get to see and talk to him, but that big red button on the bottom of the screen is a big attraction for a certain little lady who can't help but push it, so we do tend to get cut off a lot! We try to keep the kids to a routine as much as possible whether Daddy is here or if he's away, which helps. It helps me manage the kids and helps them feel secure I think.

Mark is a full time prosthetic user and hasn't used a wheelchair since June 2009. He works for the RMA (Royal Marines Association) and also travels the world as a motivational speaker. He has taken the worst situation he could face and turned it into a positive. I couldn't be any prouder of him and the inspiration he is to others; or the role model he is for our children.

" My Daddy trains people to " climb Mountains.

Abbie, 7

Planning a future of dreams without plans
Claudia, Royal Marine Girlfriend

The realisation that the person you love most in life belongs to the Corps, is quite a tough thing to come to terms with. His life must revolve around the Marines and so, by default yours does too. Planned weekends all fall by the wayside, because something has come up at work. There are times that you need someone the most and they have no means of communication; when the big things in life happen and you often find yourself dealing with them as a single person. It is difficult but you just have to get your head around it from the beginning. For me it was a case of realising this was all part of being with a Royal Marine and I just have to accept all the things that come with the job. I made the choice early on and although it is never, ever, easy, you learn how to no longer plan and instead just let things happen.

One of the most overwhelmingly proud moments of my life was being able to see my man at his Passing Out Parade. It was unforgettable. Just to talk about it brings tears to my eyes. The way he looked, where he stood, how he marched; it will always be one of the most memorable moments of my life. It was a long time coming and I honestly couldn't think of someone who deserved it more. The journey to get to that point had been one of many highs and lows. Although you're at home, you still go through the process with them. I remember just waiting for those phone calls or messages to say he'd passed another test or got through another exercise, despite his feet and joints being strapped up beyond recognition. It was one of the most turbulent experiences I have ever been through but to get to see the Kings Squad Pass Out was such a reward for all that hard work.

My brother is also a Royal Marine and you have to choose to dedicate yourself to getting through it and remember all of the original reasons you joined. Both my brother and my fiancé were so dedicated to getting to the end of training, and to finally get a Green Beret, that it was all they focused on. If you are going to do it, live it, breathe it.

When you fall in love with someone in the Marines, you have to make a choice about whether to follow your heart, or be able to plan your future. That choice brings lots of ups and downs, lots of responsibilities and many hard times but, ultimately, if you are with the one you love accepting his career choice only makes you stronger. You definitely need patience by the bucket load to get you through life with a Royal! You also have to be loyal and learn to love your own company. Go out and get a new hobby, take up a sport, join a club or a gym. Being your own person makes the time apart a hell of a lot easier. Try not to lose your identity in the "madness" of marrying into the military.

Communication is key in any relationship but this isn't always possible for us of course. But when you can and if you need to, try to talk, really talk and listen to each other.

And last but not least, maybe get a dog!

I remember once going to a bar with one of my friends and after some general conversation, my friend decided it was a good time to let the group know my other half was a Marine. At this point I remember one of the men in the group asking me if that was true and I said "yes". He turned to me and said "That is a pretty big decision to be with someone like that, are you sure that is what you want for your life?" And I remember at that moment knowing that yes, it was very much what I wanted for my life. My fiancé is without a doubt the person for me and his career is a part of who he is. I wouldn't want him any other way.

For me the positives of our lifestyle have always outweighed the negatives but it has never been easy. I believe that the loyal wives and girlfriends of Royal Marines are some of the strongest women that I've ever met. Never underestimate how important you are as the "one who stays home".

It isn't all romantic homecomings and love letter exchanging; it is hard, hard, work.

For me our future is exciting. Once you get past the lack of 'plan-ability', it becomes exciting to dream. You don't know all the places you'll go, people you'll meet and experiences you'll have. For me I choose to be excited for that.

"I have a teddy with Daddy's voice that I have had since I was born, it stops me feeling sad."

Abbie, 7.

HMS HEROES

Sat Nav Survivor

Jo. Royal Navy Wife

I was raised with two brothers by my Mum and Dad until the age of eleven when my Mum left my Dad. We moved in with my Grandma where things were a little bit of a squeeze but we managed, most of the time, to get along. I had to share a bedroom with my Mum which was challenging at times especially as I went into my teenage years with mood swings and all that. But it was the making of our relationship not only as Mother and Daughter but as friends who greatly respected each other. My Mum is my best friend and no matter what life throws my way she will always be there for me.

I met my husband through a mutual friend and we dated for a year before we had to make a huge decision about our life. I lived in the Midlands and he is based with The Royal Navy in Plymouth. If our relationship was to move forward we had to make some choices. It wasn't an easy decision to leave my Mum and the rest of my family behind but the decision we came to, was that I would join him in Plymouth and that's when I became part of the Royal Navy family. I moved here in 2008, two days before my husband was deployed for six months. I had no job, no friends and not a clue where anything was. I felt stranded and abandoned. But I am not someone who will sit and feel sorry for myself. You just have to get on with things.

That deployment took some time getting used to as I wasn't able to just call my Husband and he was also away for Christmas. At times it was very lonely.

I was once told "you knew what you were getting yourself in for" but NO you don't!! And to say it gets easier the more they go away is not true either. I survived that first deployment and got a job, a choice of three jobs in fact, and I had learnt to find my way around Plymouth far better than my husband, thanks to Sat Nav!

We are a family now with two beautiful children, born fourteen months apart. We live in married quarters and to help me cope with deployments, which are going to be a regular part of our future, I joined a 'Band of Wives' group. We learnt to recognise our own strength and coping strategies to help the children; and for me, when times are tough, I know I have ladies to lean on. I have also set up and run a coffee morning now to offer my support to other wives, who might be struggling, or who just need a chat.

I truly believe that as a military wife you have to have a lot of love for the man you are married to. Know how to work the 'Sat Nav', be able to find the strength to be without them for long periods of time and to take on whatever life throws at you; to be not only a Mum but a Dad as well.

"Mummy is like a Dr, helping people and Daddy has a," gun.

Tyler, 6.

Living a life unexpected

Steph, Royal Marine Wife

When my (then) boyfriend joined the Royal Marines I was lost, excited, and a whole bundle of emotions. Our daughter had only just turned one and on families day I noticed that I appeared to be the only one with a child. Speaking to other wives, it became apparent that many of the others had a 'ready-made Bootneck', having met their partners after they started training. But I knew my boyfriend before he had started. So I had mine from the beginning, and the training was tough! We barely saw him and the predicted thirty two weeks ended up being sixteen months due to two injuries. On the day he was meant to pass out with his original troop, he proposed to me. A few weeks later, we found out that I was pregnant again with our second child.

So many people have said to me that they didn't know how I did it; some expressed doubts about whether they thought he would actually make it, and 'pass out' of training to become a Royal Marine. But him not making it or becoming a Royal Marine didn't even cross my mind; I just knew he'd do it.

At his Kings Squad passing out parade, I felt like a whale. I was thirty six weeks pregnant, surrounded by slim, mini skirt clad eighteen year olds, trying to stop my now two year old from running around wiping bogeys on people. I felt ridiculous, and insanely jealous of their youth, their skinny legs, and non swollen ankles.

We were married the following year and we moved away from family and friends to Taunton. It was here that I've met some incredible women. There was no concept of "wearing their husbands rank". The "WAGs" (Wives and Girlfriends) that I've met have been strong and brave and modest. You just have to "crack on" is an attitude we all seem to share.

Being part of the Royal Marines family has taught me a lot. I've found I'm less tolerant of my old friends who moan that their boyfriends are away for the weekend. But I have also learnt to bite my tongue. It's all relative isn't it? I miss my husband more than I can put into words when he's away but as soon as he's home, he drives me up the wall. Absence really does make the heart grow fonder. I don't think we'd know how to be a "normal" family now.

Everyday I'm proud; I'm proud of him for doing it, for excelling, for going after his dream and not letting go, despite injuries and setbacks. I'm proud of our strong daughters who miss their Daddy. Of course there are always tears but they are so brave and just wipe those tears away. They support me just as much as I support them; they keep me strong. My eldest is only three but I couldn't have done this without her. She's my strength, and my baby is my little clown; she makes me laugh when I want to cry. When I'm scared, her cheeky face lets me know that us girls will be just fine until Daddy comes home.

And ultimately I'm proud of me, for adapting to the life pretty well, I think, although I feel like I've aged about forty years. I'm proud to be part of the family although it's not a life I ever expected for myself.

"When Daddy comes home I try to show him a surprise."

Jason, 5

Puzzle Pieces

Louise, Royal Marine Wife

I met my husband Michael, in June 2009 and it was supposed to be a bit of fun, absolutely nothing more. But it turned out to be a whirlwind that turned my life upside down - for the better! There was just something more to him. He wasn't pretentious or trying to be the big Marine; although it did help that when we first met he was in 'rig' (uniform). We met a few times when he had his time off from 'behind the wire' (being on camp).

At one point we even had the "what the hell are we doing and where is it going?" chat; both of us had thought of ending the relationship because we realised that we were falling for each other and neither of us were in that place of wanting it. We never knew at the time but we'd both written a message ending things, but never actually sent it.

After such a short space of time, in August 2009, we decided that there really was no turning back. We had already decided to move in together and buy somewhere. Deciding to be with Michael and give the relationship a chance was the best thing I ever did and I have never looked back.

At this point I went from the least maternal woman who was terrified of children to feeling really broody. I think this is when I knew he was the one. It felt like a jigsaw just fitted together perfectly all of a sudden. I was a bit scared to admit my feelings though, as it all happened so suddenly, but by now I realised he's not easily frightened off! So, just seven months after we first met, we found out we were expecting our first baby.

I find it very hard to trust. Michael says I had a wall around me, but he could see that it wasn't really me; I was hiding a lot inside. I read something once that said "I don't build walls to keep people out but to see who will climb over them". It is so true for me. It took a lot for me to accept that when he was away from me, I just had to put my complete trust in him.

Three years after meeting, now with a toddler and baby, we got married. He proposed on his two weeks R and R (Rest and Relaxation) from Afghanistan, in 2012. Our wedding day was the most special, intimate and personal day and I loved everything about it; it was completely about us. Definitely the most rewarding highlight of our story was this day. We had been through him being posted to the other end of the country, Afghanistan, his Mum dying soon after, then the birth of our second child before finally we got our happy ever after. But after everything we have been through, it meant so much more.

I have a picture hanging in my house that says – 'Sometimes the dreams that come true are the dreams you never even knew you had'. I absolutely didn't imagine I'd be happy as a housewife, self employed, fundraising for charity and being actively involved in the Royal Marines, with three little children and moving all over the country. But I am absolutely the happiest and most content I've ever been. It all feels right, I have a purpose and I can be myself completely. I don't need to shut anything out, hide anything away or feel silly about talking. And it makes me a better person having experienced it all.

I met my husband when he was already in the Royal Marines so this is all I know. When he comes home from work he is Dad and husband and it is important to separate. However, I am interested in his work and what's going on, being actively involved with Royal Marines Association and Royal Marines Charitable Trust Fund and Trim4Veterans; a volunteer programmes offering specific, structured support for veterans. I know some wives who absolutely draw a line and don't really want to get involved with the Corps. If that works for them, great! For us, we are genuinely best mates as well as Husband and Wife. If he wants to chat, I can detach myself to do that. What I think is important, is that you have to understand that the man you marry may be the most reliable and grounded person but their job isn't. It sounds harsh but you need to just accept that with no questions. Decisions which directly impact your life are out of your hands. What is the most important thing for our family is being together. I have done 'unaccompanied drafts' and now married 'accompanied drafts' living on a 'married patch'. If it means moving every year, we will do it. My children are four, three and two. The most important thing is having all of us together. We are a team and support each other and the best thing for us is being together as much as possible. We are all absolutely lost if one of the pieces of the puzzle is missing. We can function but it doesn't feel right.

I know that my family question our lifestyle and our decision to bring children into it. However, my kids are very grounded. They have experienced a whole range of things in their short lives and perhaps have grown up quickly because of it.

We don't countdown because the last thing I want is to build up to a homecoming that doesn't happen, and I know how often homecomings are delayed or changed. We write a diary every day (well I do and they tell me what they want to say) so my Husband can catch up with what he has missed. It's more or less the conversation we'd have about the day once he gets in from work. We also have a map and globe and put flags showing where we all are. It's hard for everyone, but I find that my children are very accepting as long as I'm absolutely truthful with them; I speak to them as an equal. When it comes to moving, in all honesty their opinion, along with mine, is often irrelevant, particularly if we're drafted to meet the Corps needs rather than through our own choice. But we still discuss it, as it affects us all. I find military kids are incredibly switched on. Some families tell them everything, some shelter them. Personally, we discuss everything because they are so young, they just accept it.

My husband is away now and missed our sons fourth birthday which was hard for me. My son decided himself that he didn't want a big birthday but a Halloween party because Dad would be home then. He often talks about what we will do when Dad's home and what he will do for me because I've been working hard (unfortunately for him he still needs a hand to follow it through). I try not to show my feelings if I'm upset because I don't want them to get upset too. However, if it happens, my four year old is very perceptive and gives me a hug telling me we're a team and we're all best friends. It's heartbreaking but they absolutely accept the job, the consequences of war, and can point out Afghanistan on a map!

"I am sad when Daddy is away. But I know he has to and I'm happy that he eams money for us."

Jaden, 8.

Love over the 'Landline'

Adele, former Royal Navy Wife

Being an older Navy wife, I look back at how my, now grown up, sons coped with their Dad (a submariner) preparing to deploy.

The boys were aged around ten and five years old, I would give them a countdown to Dad deploying to prepare them and keep it as a normal part of our lives, which of course it was. On the day he was due to leave, I would wake them early and wrap them up, and bundle them into the car in their PJ's and slippers to drop their Dad off. Submarines always leave at some un-godly hour in the morning. We would drive to the dockyard with the boy's faces slowly dropping. They would cry all the way home. However, submarines being submarines and always breaking down, he would be home by teatime!

A few days later I would go through the same routine again, and, as before, the boys would cry, but not as much as they did the first time. By the third attempt we would again be on that familiar road to the dockyard, hug, say goodbye and wave, as I would pull away to drive home. This time the journey would be in silence, two sets of dry eyes. Eventually the youngest would ask "Mummy do you think he has really gone this time?" This uncertainty would shape the first few days and weeks, as they expected him to be home in time for tea. I would meet them from school and watch as their eyes momentarily looked past me, just in case, then flicker as they turned back to focus on just me with a watery smile.

Normality for them would be keeping to their daily routines; communication was almost non-existent with their Dad. We didn't count down the days as there was no clear date for any return; if the deployment was 'silent' which meant no contact for several weeks, for them, it was as if he had disappeared from their lives. More often than not there would be a cryptic message on the landline to let me know that they were due home or, just to add a bit of excitement into my day, a message, "Can you call this telephone number for important information regarding your husband"!

I guess each generation of military wives can look to the new, younger fresh -faced wives and smile knowingly as they hear them complain at not having daily contact with their loved one. In my younger days communication did not include e-mails, mobiles sending text messages, leaving voice messages,

Facebook, twitter or other social media – it just didn't exist!! Paradigm[9] anda free twenty minute call was just a fantasy! And I'm only talking about the late seventies, and eighties. I am going back to the days of good old fashioned letter writing. That meant spending hours in WH Smiths choosing the right paper and colour; Basildon Bond if you could afford it and matching envelopes. Each letter would be dated as you filled it with the joys of your daily lives, sprayed with perfume and sealed with a lipstick kiss with S.W.A.L.K (sealed with a loving kiss) written on the back. On the front you would number the letter so that when your letters arrived in bulk, he would know what order to open them in.

Oh the excitement when a letter would finally arrive for me. I remember watching the postman as he walked down the road, ready to rugby-tackle him for his precious cargo. I remember the disappointment when he walked past without looking at you, as you wiped away a tear. You told yourself never mind there's always tomorrow and then, finally the click of the letterbox as it plopped onto the carpet; my heart would lurch! Is it from him? I'd rush to pick it up, turning it over to check if he signed it with anything, look at the postmark to see where it was posted, and then finally, carefully open it, and find somewhere to sit to read it over and over again. Young love! As I received my letters, once read I would pile them into bundles wrapped in ribbon to keep in a box under the bed to be brought out and re-read if I was feeling lonely, or when I felt abandoned, as though his return was never going to come around.

There also used to be 'Familygrams' – No bad news, no codes, nothing contentious - just utter blandness! Don't mention the dog's accident, no saucy comments, no reference to old arguments or broken cars, no words of undying love. Remember who else is reading it. All in forty words or less!

As I waited for the phone to ring I'd be weighing up the probabilities of him phoning during the day, do I go out and do the shopping? Take the boys to school clubs? Or remain trapped in the house sat by a phone that never rings? If I risked going out, you could guarantee that the minute I got back the light would be flashing with a message; "I'm trying to ring you, we are only here for a few hours!" I could tell by his tone he wasn't impressed at my lack of commitment to phone sitting. I could always tell when he had

---

9 Paradigm is a free service providing a 20 or 30 minute phone card.

landed somewhere and was trying to contact us. The phone would ring and as I rushed to answer it, it would click click click then go dead … this would happen several times over a few hours before finally an angry voice shouting "hello, hello" would snap into the handset. The first few minutes taken up with the complaints of a fed up submariner in Scotland walking from telephone box to telephone box, trying to find one that worked, and wasting his money as each one swallowed his coins, running out of change. The joy as the shrill tone of the telephone shatters the night's silence, dragging you out of a deep sleep at stupid o'clock, and a drunken voice slurs down the phone – and you try to make sense of the conversation and reply … *nicely*. Despite knowing you have to be up in two hours to take the children to school, all the while knowing that he is in a posh hotel enjoying a few beers with the lads. It's a hard life in a blue suit.

> ❞ When Daddy is away I feel sad and I keep forgetting that he has gone away.
>
> Austin, 4.

Nostalgia is a beautiful thing, but believe me when I say military wives are made of sterner stuff.

Emily, HMS HEROES

A Decent Proposal

Alex, Royal Marine Wife

The journey of being a 'WAG' or married to the Marines has been quite interesting to say the least, with a wedding, deployments, children, distance and promotions to name just a few of the stops along the way.

You may ask how we all do it. Well, you have to be a certain kind of person to be with a 'Bootneck'. Royal Marines all have the same outlook on life and I think to some extent it does rub off on you, whether you want it to or not, even the language aka 'Bootneck speak'.

You have to be able to stand your own company for long periods of time. Be both Mummy and Daddy whilst he is away. You have to be able to pick up your own life when he goes and then just as easily, adjust back into your couple or family life when he comes home. Building a support network of friends, or other Wives and Girlfriends, is one of the biggest and most important things you need to be able to do, because these are the ones that will help you through the military life as they know exactly how you feel and what you go through. We stick together and support each other through thick and thin.

I don't know what I expected of being in a relationship with a Royal Marine, I didn't even really think about the amount of time that he would be away and where he would have to go both in terms of deployments and drafts. I just loved the fact that I was with him!

I met Bill in 2004 when l worked for the company that deals with all the hire cars for the forces. He rang me at 4.30pm on a Friday to book a ridiculous amount of minibuses for the next day and it went from there. We got chatting and one day when he called, I could hear one of the lads in the background shouting. I asked what was happening and he said that one of the lads was shouting "just ask her out will ya". I just laughed it off.

We were friends for a few months and then, as my current relationship broke down, strangely he was the person I first turned too. Not my Mum or best friend but this 6ft tall, Royal Marine, who had become my friend and confidante. We finally got together Christmas 2004 but he then went off on leave back to his Mum's and I didn't see him until he briefly

45

came back to work in January. He then, almost immediately, went away on exercise that first week of January and didn't come home until March. When he came back he literally didn't leave my flat so I gave him a key and that was that. As soon as he brought his first lot of dirty washing around I knew he wasn't leaving. We had talked about getting married pretty much from the start and even went ring shopping. I got a call at work from him one day asking what time I would be home and would I definitely be home at that time. I was like "Yes, I will be home at five."

As I pulled up to our flat the curtains were closed, the curtains were never closed in the day. I walked into the flat shouting "Hiya I'm home" and turned the corner into our front room to find him in his Dress Blues on one knee holding the engagement ring, with a banner on the wall that he made himself, asking whether I would marry him. I said yes and we got married six months later in a small wedding on the Isle of Man. They are romantics really in their own way, they don't like to admit it, but they are.

He used to tell me stories of when he was in Northern Ireland, the stuff that had happened to him. To be honest I think because I hadn't known him then, it didn't feel real. It soon got real when he came home in September 2006 and told me that he was off to Afghanistan. Obviously I'd seen it in the news and knew what was happening but it didn't even occur to me that he would go. Looking back now I realise how naive I was. We prepared as much as you can prepare to be apart for six months. It's a long time to be apart and you can't even really imagine it until you have lived through it. Bill is a strong character and I think that has rubbed off on me. I took my strength from him. The night came that he deployed, we were at camp waiting for the coach to come and get them and he kept asking me "Are you ok? Are you ok?" I was like "yeah, I'm fine, don't worry about Me." but inside I was just about holding it together. He got on the coach waving goodbye. Once the coach had gone from view I sat in the car alone and that was when I broke down. Just me on my own. The feeling that a piece of me had just left and honestly the reality hit me, whether I would ever get to see him again. As dramatic as that sounds it was the honest truth.

The tour went pretty smoothly from both our points of view. I got my head together and got into a routine. The first week was pretty pants

I'm not going to lie but then I found ways of getting through it. I had a countdown chart at work, I worked out how many days he was out there for, which I think was about 180 days and then I would cross one day off each morning I went into work. Mondays were the best as I got to cross off three days at once. I used to send a box a week out to him; I went to the post office and bought 24 boxes, to post out sweets, favourite food, toiletries, and little gifts to boost morale. That was another way of counting down the weeks; I could see how many boxes were left. Eblueys[10] are a fabulous thing, especially when you get one back from him. We didn't have Facebook or Skype or anything like that when he was first there. It literally was eblueys and sometimes email. Oh and the best phone calls ever.

The tour eventually ended and it was time for him to come home. I remember driving to camp so excited but also so nervous. I hadn't seen my husband in six months, would he look the same? How would he be with me? All that didn't matter when I saw him getting off the coach, I walked slowly to him and he picked me up and spun me around and I think I might have cried just a little, but don't tell anyone.

He was home, he was safe and he was with me. I realised that I had survived the deployment in more ways than one, a stronger person and a bit readier to survive another one down the line.

He just wanted it to be the same at home, but of course I had been alone for six months and had got myself into a new routine and it does take some adjustment on both parts to get back to "normal". The lads have a de-brief about how to adjust to being at home again, but there wasn't anything for families, we just had to deal with it as best we could. Bill was quieter and more thoughtful when he came home for quite a few months after his tour. I asked him to tell me about things but he just said that he was ok and I didn't need that in my head. I just made sure that he knew if he wanted to talk he could - about anything and at any time. After about six months, he seemed more like his old self but he was still changed. I suppose I should have expected the change, you

---

10 'Blueys' are the nickname for military letters as they are written on blue airmail paper. Eblueys are a quicker way to send a letter- you would type your letter and upload photos in the same way as an email, but it would be printed off by military personnel in the destination country, in this case Camp Bastion, and then posted onto the recipient. It could shorten the postage time to just three days instead of three weeks.

can't expect them to go out there and not come back a little different andI will never know fully what happened out there. I am just thankful that he came back full stop.

Life eventually went back to normal, both of us back to work. We bought our first house and were so excited and then found out in August 2008 that I was pregnant with our first child. Within the same week we also found out he was being deployed back to Afghanistan. That was quite an emotional tour: I blame the hormones! Off he went in September, leaving me just about holding it together again. My first scan was in October, I was sat in the waiting room looking around at all the happy smiling Mummy and Daddies to be. It made me a little sad that I was here on my own with Bill thousands of miles away. As soon as I saw the scan I cried, the lady asked where my partner was and I replied Afghanistan. She must have felt sorry for me because she printed out about six pictures for me so that I could send them to him. Every week I sent a picture through the ebluey system of how my tummy was growing.

R and R (Rest and Relaxation) came around, I picked him up from camp and as he got off the coach again I ran at him this time and jumped on him at six months pregnant, the first thing he did was drop to his knees and kiss my tummy. When he had left I had no tummy, he came home and I was massive. I am one of the very lucky ones as he was home in more than enough time for the birth but that one was a hard emotional tour. He lost friends, lots of things happened, and I once again had to deal with the adjustment of him being home and also me being pregnant. He didn't let me out of his sight for a while and was making sure that my bump was protected when we were out. As hard and tough as Royal Marines are, they are very soft at heart. The day he left to go back to Afghanistan for the remainder of the tour was pretty tough.

It seems a long time waiting for the immense sense of relief that goes through you when he finally calls from Cyprus to say that he has left Afghanistan and will be on his way home in a few days. Then the call to say that they are in UK is even better and I cannot even put into words how you feel. He didn't have to be home, I was just so excited that he was back in the country. And safe.

When my son was ten months old, Bill was drafted to another part of the country and we decided that I would stay in Plymouth and he would be a "weekend warrior". At the time this was the right decision, however looking back Bill missed out on so much with our first son. First steps, first words... In the July of that year I found out I was pregnant again - with twins.

This time I knew that I would have to move to be with him and be together as a family, so I moved into married quarters. I actually told him we were having twins over the telephone, things like that you don't think about, you presume that your partner will be around for you to share that incredible moment when you find out you are having a baby but it's just another thing to deal with when your partner is in the military. He missed all scans with both pregnancies and I know deep down he is a bit disappointed that he didn't get to go to them.

It always makes me feel a little jealous when I meet people who have their family right on the door step. Ours live five hours away and although we all visit regularly, it's not the same as having your Mum right down the road. Especially when the deployments come and all you want is a cuddle from your Mum. That's something that people take for granted, I appreciate Mum and Dad so much more as I don't get to see them as much as I would want to.

I get all the time from friends, "Oh I don't know how you do it" or the common one "I couldn't do it". Well, of course you could do it if you met the person you wanted to be with. It makes me mad that my civilian friends are not as understanding as they could be. To be honest that's probably why I have more military friends than civilian now. People can also be very rude, which I never experienced until recently. Comments like "I don't agree with the soldiers being there" and "they are over there illegally". Regardless of whether you are for, or against the war in Afghanistan, have respect for all those out there doing their job and think before you speak because you have no idea what that person in front of you is going through at that moment. Some people just really do not have a clue about military families and what we go through on a daily basis.

As Wives and Girlfriends there is a certain amount of things that you know you will have to put up with, like distance, deployment, lots of travelling to see them, but what you don't get told is the moving every two years to a house that isn't yours. You spend so much time making it home and then you pack up and you're off again, leaving the friends that you have made along the way. You then have to start all over again, moving, unpacking, making new friends. I get told the age old saying of "well you knew what you were getting yourself into when you married him". Well, No! Actually I didn't think about the whole moving your entire life around the country to keep your family together and to make sure that your kids get to see Daddy.

However, all this being said, why would I want a 9-5 hubby when I have a real life Royal Marine, where would be the fun in that? I cannot express enough how much love and pride I have for this one man and everything that has happened and all that we have achieved together.

"My Daddy is a Royal Marine. He is my Hero."

Seth, 5

50

my
diddy
a
hefo

Seth, 5

Living his Dream

Chearyl, Royal Marine Wife

Ben and I have been together twelve years now. When we first met he was on course to enlist within the forces but he pulled out of it as he was only seventeen at the time, and we had just met. He knew that I wasn't keen.

Over the years we became a proper couple, had full time careers and at twenty two, we had our first baby.

It was around this time that I could see that Ben was terribly unhappy with his career path. He was a full time scaffolder and although he earned very decent money he was forever doing his best, but not getting any recognition. He believed, and I knew too, that he was meant to do something greater and more fulfilling.

It wasn't until after our second baby two years later, that Ben told me that he had been looking into joining the Royal Marines again but he was going to do it as a reservist. I absolutely hated the idea and talked him out of it.

We were happy, but there was something niggling in our relationship and home life. He would often come home depressed and it had a huge impact on our family time together. We married in 2000. It was the happiest day of our lives but there was still this undercurrent in our lives of how miserable my Husband was in his career.

I watched him as he continued to put himself on courses to succeed and climb the ladder, yet it only created more work for himself. He would wake every morning in a foul mood to set off and do his 'duty as a man' and provide for us. Again, the topic came up about him wanting to fulfil his dream of wearing a green beret and, again, I shot him down. But this time he had taken it a step further and started the enquiries that were involved with him achieving this. His family sat him down and talked him out of it, telling him to stay with us and not to embark on "that" life…

It was after this that the rows started and the resentment towards me. Things went from bad to worse and I asked my husband to leave our marital home. It was an awful, horrid time in our lives, especially as I had just found out that I was carrying our third child.

Finally I realised, it was time for me to take a step back and to stop being selfish. I had to make some decisions; did I let our family fall apart or did

I take the risk of letting him fulfil his dreams? Stand by him and let him create a new outcome for us? I wanted my marriage to work and so I called him, he came over and I told him that if we were going to stay together then he had to try and fulfil his dream of being a Royal Marine Commando but not part time. If he was going to do it then he had to do it properly, and I would support him.

At thirty weeks pregnant I clutched my three and five year olds hands and sobbed my heart out as he left to embark on his thirty two weeks training.

I next saw Ben when I was thirty four weeks pregnant. I drove the 130 miles with our children to Exeter for families' day and I bought him home for the weekend. The next time I would see him would be when I was delivering our third child.

To prevent him from getting 'back trooped' (kept behind in training) but also to try and ensure he would be at the birth. I made the hard decision to have an elective c-section. He would only get to have three days with us, before continuing his training.

Our baby had to be placed in special care and Ben had to leave us at the hospital. Luckily I had my Mother around to help take care of the older children. I sobbed so hard when he said goodbye to us in the hospital. But I also knew it was hard for him to walk away. He wanted to leave training and be a "normal" family again and as much as I wanted to beg him to quit, I knew he would hate himself eventually for it.

Seven days after my c-section I was at home with our three children, my Mum had left and I was all alone. I had to register the birth and had no one around to drive me so I got in the car and drove, then I had to haul the pram and car seat about and walk some distance, even though I was still in pain from the surgery, but I knew I just had to get on with things. I think it hit me hard then; what we had committed to... but at the same time I realised I could do this.

The thirty two week training that the men endure is not just for them, it's also for the families they leave behind. It gives a true representation of what life will be like in the Corps.

I had extremely low days, looking back over my diary entries I think I may have been suffering with Post Natal Depression at times. When I did get the opportunity to speak to my Husband he forever doubted himself, and was extremely tired and run down from the hard training he was going through. I could not sit there and cry to him because I had to push him through, constantly reminding myself that we have done all this for a reason.

When our baby was six weeks old Ben had his three weeks summer leave and we had the most amazing time together. I loved having him back in my life. I was falling in love, all over again, with my husband.

When he had to return to training things got hard again only this time it was the effect on the older children and even the dog.

The children were missing him and finding it hard now, they had lost their Daddy and gained a brother. We had also had to part with our oldest dog as he was would not be getting the attention he needed with Ben away. He went to live with family, so we still saw him but it was something else to add to the list of changes that we were all struggling to come to terms with.

It was actually the older children that got us through, especially the oldest. I remember him having a conversation with Ben on the phone and telling him he could do it and to not give up.

I was shouting all the time and feeling so stressed out and generally like an awful Mother. They would sob and pine for their Dad and then I would be in pieces. Once, when he had been on a long weekend home (which is never really a long weekend) our four year old literally clung to his leg screaming "don't leave" I had to prize him away. He had bad dreams and started to wet himself at school. Our six year old was always angry but wouldn't explain why, until one day he literally exploded in front of Ben screaming "I hate you so much".

Saying "goodbye" all the time was the hardest thing and it never gets any easier.

Throughout his time away I had no one to really speak to, that was going through the same thing. In an online forum, I found a girl whose Husband was also due to pass out soon. She was pregnant and had a child, so she really guided me through the experience and it was so good to vent to someone who knew exactly how I was feeling. We eventually met and our Husbands were based in the same unit. She now lives local to me and we are good friends. I will never forget how she helped pull me through those training days. I have also met a group of the other WAGs locally and with online communities. They are all lovely and there is a real bond we share. We always know how to pull each other through.

It is a part of this Corps life that I have learnt to cherish.

Ben passed out in January this year. He completed his training in the thirty two weeks and walked away with the PT (physical fitness) medal.

The children were so proud to watch him be crowned with his green lid. It's a moment they will never forget. By April we had relocated 130 miles, leaving everything we knew to start afresh. I thought it was going to be hard and dreaded moving the children from everything they knew particularly their school. At times it has been difficult but overall they have adapted really well and are now very settled. Our middle child has not had one bad dream or accident since the move and we are all enjoying our new life together.

Most of all though we have learnt as a family to appreciate each other and I feel like the whole experience has given us a second chance to be united and happy.

"To stop me missing Daddy, My mummy gives me kisses and my baby brother makes me laugh"

~ Beau, 6.

55

Love can conquer all

Hayley, Royal Navy Wife

My toughest battle to date was dealing with an eleven month deployment; perhaps because it's been the most recent and that's why it stands out above the rest.

During that deployment I had to deal with a few things, firstly losing my Nan, who was a big part of our lives; then having to cope with frequent hospital visits, due to our then fifteen month old son being Asthmatic. This often resulted in overnight stays; not such an easy task when you have another child to consider and your nearest family member is nearly three hundred miles away.

I also lost my cousin during this deployment which was an incredibly tough time as she left behind a daughter just six months younger than my own.

These were a few of the extra hardships on top of the fact that I'd more or less become a single parent of two small children and dealing with the day to day stresses that brings. I often look back and wonder how I coped with it all and can only attribute that to having the support of good friends.

I think this lifestyle teaches you a great deal about yourself and your relationship, but, without meaning to sound self righteous, it's not for the faint hearted and you have to truly love them or it's not worth going through with it. Because there will be times when you will want to throw in the towel, times when you get fed up of sleeping alone, times when your heart aches for them, times when you can't help but think this is what it would be like if the worst was to happen. You will feel emotions you never thought possible!

But you will also feel the renewed excitement when they are due to return, the pride in believing your love can conquer all, the feeling of being a teenager in love when you run down the gangway into each other's arms. A sense of pride when you watch them march in remembrance day parades and the feeling you get when you watch your children run into theirs Daddies arms is one I simply have no words for.

Our relationship has been tested to the extremes but we've made it through and we're also still laughing! That is a common occurrence in our house, we regularly, all four of us, when Daddy is home, have tickle fights; which normally ends up with me and the kids pinning Daddy down and tickling him until he cries for surrender!

Oliver, 6

"Me and my family watch the ships on the telly and pretend it is Daddy on his way home.

Lucy, 10

Transatlantic Love

Claire, Royal Marine Wife

O ur story begins in 2010. I was a 23-year-old girl living in Jacksonville, Florida. I worked at a specialty tea shop and all my life consisted of was going to the beach, bars, and clubs. I had nothing else to worry about. I met Andrew that summer at an Irish bar on the beach. I had been at the beach all day and was still wearing my bikini and cover-up. My make-up had washed off and my hair was a beachy mess. I was waiting for a friend to finish work and meet me there. As I was waiting, I was approached by a guy with an accent, I can't remember exactly the first thing he said to me, but I batted him off with some sarcastic remark – I wasn't really in the mood to be hit on. His come-back was equally sarcastic and then it just became a battle in banter.

He and some more of his friends were leaving the bar to go to a house party. They invited me to join them and Andrew and I ended up sitting on a sun lounger by the side of the communal pool, talking about life and what we wanted out of it. We both spoke of wanting to travel the world and I guess we just started ticking all of each other's boxes. At one point he jokingly asked me to marry him having no idea that one day I would.

The night ended with me taking him and three of the lads to McDonald's and then back to Mayport where they were stationed at the time. Before Andrew got out of the car, he asked for my number and when it got to the part where he had to put my name in, he couldn't remember what my name was, but, to be fair, I couldn't remember his. We laughed about that and then I went home. Within two minutes of walking in my front door, I got a call from him and he 'just wanted to chat'. We talked on the phone for about an hour before saying good night and falling asleep as it was about five am by this point. I got a text message the next morning from him, and all it said was, 'just in case'. I think he was worried that I would forget about him. I didn't see him for another week and a half, but we texted and talked on the phone all that time. After that first week or so, we spent the rest of his time in Jacksonville with each other.

Every. Single. Day.

We fell so hard for each other; I had never felt anything like it before in my life. We were so alike, it was scary – we were both gingers, as well! Little did I know that my life was about to drastically change, and it was all because of this Royal Marine I met at a beach bar.

Andrew's ship took off four weeks after I met him, and that's when I realized our little summer fling meant a lot more when we said our goodbyes. It was so hard to say goodbye - I almost felt like he was dying and I was never going to see him again! I had fallen in Love with him and I could tell he had done the same with me. He was continuing his tour in Brazil and then was going to be heading back to England. We kept in touch through email, Skype, whatsapp, and text, throughout the rest of his deployment. I'm so grateful for modern technology!

When we found out exactly when he'd be back in the UK, I purchased plane tickets and we planned a little trip during the two weeks leave he'd get. I just had to see him again! So, I met him in London where we spent one night, then flew to Prague the next day. We spent a week there and then five days in Edinburgh. It felt like a little honeymoon and I was only falling more and more in love with him. This was the beginning of our back-and-forth, long distance relationship.

Things were going great; he came over to the States every time he had leave. My family had also fallen in love with him and helped pay for his plane tickets to come over as often as he could.

At Christmas 2011 we went to South Africa together so that I could meet his family – he's originally from South Africa, his parents split when he was a baby and when he was fifteen he moved to England to live with his Dad. I met his Mom, Sister, and the most important man in his life, his 'Oupa', his name for Grandfather. When we got back from South Africa, we decided to move in together and see if we could make our relationship work actually living together.

I quit my job, left my family, the beach, and Florida weather to move to Yeovil, England. In January! - I gave no thought to the sunshine and everything else I was leaving behind; none of that mattered because I would be with the person I loved the most.

This is when things began to get real. When I came over, I brought what little savings I had, knowing that on a six month tourist visa, I wouldn't be able to work. We lived in a really tiny flat in Yeovil which cost half of his wages each month. We barely got by and there was always way too much month at the end of our money. Naturally, this put a strain on things. What couple doesn't argue about money? I also didn't know anybody so my only human contact was Andrew. He would go to work during the day, and I would stay at home watching 'Come Dine with Me' and other trash TV. I even started playing Skyrim on his Play Station 3. I was so bored! I absolutely hated when he went on exercise because that would mean that however long he was away for, would be an uninterrupted period of loneliness for me.

And the rain! It rains all the time! For someone who comes from the Sunshine State, this was really depressing for me. When I would ask him why we never hung out with any of his friends, he would tell me that everybody went home - wherever their home was on the weekends. I started to resent him and wished that we could trade places – that I was the one who went to work every day, and he stayed home by himself. I don't think he understood how bad it really was for me then. I felt underappreciated for what I had sacrificed to be with him.

I cried almost every day and couldn't wait for the end of our six month trial period. Then something happened that would change things quite a bit. I found out I was pregnant. It terrified me, I was only twenty four and Andrew and I weren't getting along – not to mention there was no way we could afford to have a baby. Sadly, I ended up miscarrying at 11 weeks. I blamed Andrew immediately, cruelly saying it was his fault I lost the baby. I told him that stress and depression can end pregnancies and I know how cruel this was because it wasn't his fault. We could've been the happiest couple alive and it could have still happened. But, in my anger and grief, I blamed his job for keeping him away all the time.

It's so different handling them being away when you're in a familiar place. It was easier for me to cope with the distance when I was surrounded by family, friends, and a job in Florida. Now that I was alone and didn't know anybody, it was a completely different ball game. Those six months were some of the darkest in our relationship but somehow our love was strong enough that we persevered.

The night before I left to go back home to the States, Andrew showed a part of himself I had never seen before. He sobbed for hours about how badly he had messed up the previous six months and how worried he was that he wouldn't ever see me again after I got on that plane. I told him that after almost two years of enduring a long distance relationship and then getting through the hardest six months of my life, I still loved him more than anything and I wasn't going anywhere. We made the decision that night that I would apply for a fiancé visa upon arrival in the States. Everybody thought I was an absolute lunatic for doing this, but love makes you do crazy, crazy things! A week after being home, I discovered I was pregnant again. When I called Andrew to tell him, he couldn't be happier. So we went with it, knowing I'd spend most of my pregnancy in the States away from him while my fiancé visa was being processed.

This all happened summer 2012, the summer of the London Olympics; the lads did security for the event and he would also be on ship. So, I knew that contact would be sporadic and limited. It was difficult getting the documents I needed for the visa with an ocean between us and the Olympics only added to the challenge. In between the Olympics and the ships deployment, he had just two weeks leave. He came to visit me in the States, and to attend the sex scan of our baby. Seeing his face as he watched his baby boy for the first time on that screen was something I'd never forget. You could tell it was instant love.

We had an amazing couple of weeks and I was sad to see him go but by now, leaving and saying goodbye were nothing new for us.

There is something every person about to start a relationship in the forces should know. If you don't 100% trust your other half, it will never work. There are too many opportunities for that trust to be broken, and once it's broken, it's like trying to put toothpaste back in the tube after you've squeezed it out. Forces relationships aren't like normal relationships and they have to be treated differently. Other people don't realize how hard it really is and what you have to fight through. We had some big trust issues that we had to fight out on a windy beach in Jacksonville, in order to overcome them. But we had come too far, and fought too hard already, to just throw in the towel when it got tough. It actually helped our relationship reach a new level of understanding. He was finally able to notice what I had given up for him, what I would still give up for him and that I would never give up on him. On us!

Today, we have two beautiful babies; an eighteen month old boy, and a five week old girl. Things have never been better with our marriage, but there have been new hardships we've had to face. Since January of this year, Andrew has been away with work for a total of four months out of seven. He even went into work three times during his paternity leave. I have been home, alone, with two kids under the age of two for the last three weeks. I have no family and only a handful of friends that can help out. Anybody with one child knows how difficult it is by yourself, but two?! But, I have stopped taking it out on Andrew that I'm alone. I realise now that it is a part of his job.

Our relationship is about to be tested once again. After his summer leave, he deploys on ship for the third time and he won't be back until Christmas leave. We are going to the States together at the beginning of leave and I will stay there until January and then I will come back to England with him at the end of Christmas leave. I will have my family to help me with the babies and although I do trust him, it's still hard. I know I'm not the only one who feels this way before their partner goes away.

I am thankful that I have the opportunity to go the States for help, as I know not everyone has the opportunity to get help or a supportive family. But just because someone out there may have it harder than me, doesn't mean that it's still not hard.

I love Andrew with all my heart and everything that we have been through has made our relationship unbreakable. If we haven't broken by now, we never will. We have been through so much together and worked so hard to get to where we are. I have passed up so many job opportunities to support his career and stay home and make babies, but I know that when it's my turn, he will stand behind me and support me. Until then, I will continue to endure our time apart and know that it can't last forever.

"To keep my mind off my Dad when he's away I read lots of books. I feel like I'm part of the story. I become the characters in the book, so I can escape the fears of, my Dad being hurt."

Taylor, 11

HMS HEROES

"When I was four I had a globe next to my bed and I would say good night to where in the world,, Daddy was."

Jaden, 8

Soul Mate with a Catch

Ashley Royal Marine wife

I t is so typical, almost ironic, that when you meet the man of your dreams, your soul mate; there is a catch - you have to share him with the Marines.
You seem to spend life counting down the days until you see them.

I suppose this way of life does make people strong and brings people together. When I met my now husband we had only been together two months when he went away on a seven month tour of Afghan. His family were amazing, they had done this before and they took me under their wing, day by day, and helped me with the big things and the small. I'm not sure how I would have coped getting through the tour without them. I almost knew them better than him by the time he got back! So I guess this life bonds people when they have the understanding of what it is like living without a person you love – whether that is your Boyfriend, Husband, Dad, Son or Brother.

We now have a ten month old boy who is absolutely amazing, the sunshine of our lives. But he is growing up and changing so fast. With my Husband being away he is missing out on all the new things that our Son learns to do. It's upsetting for my Husband when he comes home and sees so much that he has missed out on, and of course we miss sharing it with him too. We miss out as a family together. I know growing up will be strange for our son without his Dad around all the time and it is so hard at times; bringing up a baby and also working on your own.

We seem to spend more time apart than we do together at times, but it means we really do appreciate each other and our time together. I guess it is like always staying in the honey moon phase of a relationship. The magic and excitement is still fresh when we do get to see him. Perhaps that saying "absence makes the heart grow fonder" is very true after all, even if it does make life harder at times as well.

Getting the 'Friday Feeling.'
Chloe, Royal Marine Wife.

I met my now husband over seven years ago when he was working as a waiter in a cocktail bar(!) and was a nineteen year old student at the local university. We instantly clicked and started meeting up but it took him about three months to get over the fact I was three years younger than him before we became a 'proper' couple. He was dissatisfied with University and dropped out, then spent the next few years going through various jobs; he worked as a cold caller for an energy company, was unemployed for a time and also tried working night shifts in a warehouse.

When I turned nineteen it was my turn to start at University. Tom was so moody and miserable all the time, being in another job he hated and not seeing much of a future, and I thought our relationship had run its course. I was moving on with my life and Tom was stuck doing something he hated. We had reached a 'crunch point' in our relationship, so I gave him an ultimatum to at least get off his backside and try for the job of his dreams, or we should go our separate ways. He rang whilst I was at University and told me that the job he had always wanted to do was to follow in the footsteps of his Grandad, but he had never allowed himself to think he could really do it, and that was to become a Royal Marine...

I had no idea what that was and just said "well go and do it then!" That started the long process of his application including interviews constant physical training and the big PRMC[11]. I had never seen him so driven to do something. With me having already moved away for University anyway, it didn't have too much of a direct impact on our relationship. It was good for him and I supported him fully. He obviously passed the PRMC and came home with the biggest smile and the ugliest boots I had ever seen!

The time came to wave him off, in his suit, bound for Lympstone. The first couple of months were a blur. I was enjoying University life, we had families day etc but it hadn't really impacted us, or our relationship. Then

---

11 PRMC is the pre-training test for Royal Marines. It is a four day, pre-training physical fitness and endurance test.

University started getting harder, assignments piled up, placements got demanding and reality hit. I had spent all my energy on supporting Tom and getting him through (even screaming and shouting when he was not allowed to come home!) But when I needed him, guilt stopped me from calling. He never had any decent sleep, he was constantly punished for minor slip-ups, and was physically pushed to do things he would never have believed possible. He was constantly near broken. How could I ring up and say: "Err Uni is hard......"?

That's when I first realised how things had changed. It seems so insignificant now but I remember at the time suddenly feeling very alone with everything I was doing whilst also having to be a rock for him. I really relied on my friends to listen to me rant and pretty much be the boyfriend that was never there. The one thing that kept me going through his training was the stupid thought "It will be over soon".

It was. But he then passed out, and got drafted to Scotland, something we had joked about and dreaded. I was devastated. I had never known anything like this before and simply thought how can we possibly be together when we are so far apart? But Tom tried his hardest to get back at every opportunity, spending most of his wages on petrol.

I did feel really alone. There were lots of things that I was feeling and struggling with that no one I knew could understand. Then, I stumbled across the RMWAGS calendar support group on facebook. It was the best thing that could have possibly happened. Within hours I was met with warm, kind words and assurances of how everything I was feeling was normal and typical and that there will be better times to come. I soon met up with lots of lovely ladies on one of the many "lonely valentines' evenings" and for various nights out or adventure days. I made, and still continue to make, some amazing friends through the network and that for me has been the best part of Tom's job; the social networking and sense of belonging to an exclusive community who you can literally rely on for everything from a bit of company when stuck in a random location to serious advice on a topic that is hard to discuss with those closest.

To be honest my story isn't really that exciting. Tom has never been sent to a warzone, his longest time away was three months. We don't have any children that miss Daddy. But his job brings so many sacrifices without those extra added complications; we can't plan any events as there is no such thing as guaranteed leave. We have had to cancel holidays, change the date of our wedding, miss out on our honeymoon, miss out on birthdays, anniversaries, parties, get together's, Sunday dinner, "Orange Wednesdays", "Dominoes Fridays", being able to argue on Sundays, sharing a bed, coming home to each other, all the things that other people take for granted. All the little things that are so insignificant but so important; and all the big things that we pretend are so insignificant, because they have to be for you to cope.

One event that has always stuck in my head was a Friday evening a few months into Tom's Scotland draft. I had won a big award from a teaching union for two years of hard work. I was so honoured and Tom was going to meet me at the ceremony to watch me be presented the award, and hear me give my speech. He set off from Scotland with lots of traffic but it was ok because it wasn't until later. So, I got ready, all dressed up and went for dinner. Still no Tom. Dinner had finished and various speeches started. Tom said he was thirty minutes away and looking at the schedule I was receiving my award in approx forty five minutes - cutting it fine but I only needed him to see my bit. Thirty minutes later and they called my name. I had tears in my eyes and everyone thought I was overwhelmed. But really I was gutted because Tom had missed my big moment something that for any other partner would have been so easy to get to. That was my first big disappointment and it hasn't gotten any easier being let down. You become a 'pro' at putting on a brave face on with the "I didn't want to do that anyway" kind of attitude... with only the odd crack appearing!

It's not all doom and gloom though, people talk about the Friday feeling: they have no idea of how good it feels when you find out the love of your life is on their way home! Every goodbye means the best hello. You really come to appreciate each other and make the most of what you do have. And even though you are so far apart you become so much closer to that person because you both sacrifice and struggle to make your relationship work.

My advice to those about to join the military is ensure you understand the sacrifice you are making and the sacrifice you are asking those who love you to make. If you understand and accept that - don't forget to remind them how important their sacrifice is too! The only reason I am happy to do this is because I know Tom wouldn't want to do any other job. My advice to those "marrying" into the military would be to never forget that there are some people who will cope with this better and others that will find it worse than you; respect that, because we are all different. Be supportive of others in similar situations and don't   make it into a competition of who has it worst! This life is hard for anyone.

" I get really emotional when Dad is away because he's a great Dad and, I love him to pieces. "

Lucy, 10

White Feathers
Sian, Royal Marine Fiance

I met Paul on October 14th 2007. It is a date that is etched into my memory. I was dressed in a khaki bikini, taking part in a charity fashion show at The Coal Exchange in Cardiff. I adjusted my belt and looked up at people coming off stage, nerves fluttered in my stomach as I realised it must be my turn now. I noticed Royal Marine Commandos were on stage at this fashion show, helping to raise money for a children's charity. I had worked alongside Royal Marines during my time in the Navy and there is something about them, which you learn to spot a mile away; although on this occasion they were also in uniform.

One of them was very tall with dark curly hair and green eyes, and as he came off stage I poked him in the side and told him "I used to be in the Navy." At that statement all five Marines turned around and the one I'd spoken to looked me over in my skimpy bikini and said "No! You couldn't have been! Not looking like that!" I laughed. Banter and joking between Wrens and Marines on ship was huge – which is of course why he made the statement. They then proceeded to "cheer me on" with shouting some military slang at me; telling me it was "redders[12] on stage" and they "needed a wet[13]". I went on stage and did my routine, trying not to laugh at them. I came off and got dressed for the after show party. The free champagne was flowing and before I knew it I found myself back in the middle of this circle of Marines again. I introduced myself properly to the tall guy – his name was Paul Woodland and his mates called him "Woody". He was tall, dark and handsome with greeny blue eyes and was extremely polite, which was so sweet.

The night went on and everything became a blur, probably due to the free champagne! Before I knew, it was home time. I said good bye to Woody and he asked me cheekily "Don't I get a kiss then?" Marines have a funny way of being cheeky and charming at the same time. My reply was "No! – You have to find me again if you want one." I turned and left the club.

The next few days at work Paul kept flashing into my head for no particular reason. I just kept thinking of him. Randomly one of my friends

---

12. 'Redders' is Royal Marine slang for hot.
13. 'Wet' is a Royal Marine slang term for drink

asked me if I had met a guy called Woody at the fashion show. I was shocked to find that he moved in the same circle as one of my friends, but I hadn't met him before. Once I knew this and thought there was a chance I may actually get to see him again, I couldn't resist looking him up on social media.

To my horror I found out he had just flown out to Afghanistan. I thought that would probably end any chance of getting to know him, I assumed we would have no communication and our lives would just go their separate ways. Having been in the military myself I knew communication during deployment was intermittent; I understood that it could be weeks, if not months without speaking to family, let alone a girl he barely knew. But I still couldn't stop thinking about him and, as he was in Afghanistan, I took the plunge and sent him a message on his social media, to wish him well. And every day after that I went to the library to use their Wi-Fi to check my messages. Four days later I got a reply:

"Hey Sian thanks for the msg. put a smile on my dusty, sand covered face.

Yeah was a little gutted couldn't make it to the other after show party thing. Sadly I couldn't get a taxi from Afghan to Cardiff!?

All is good with me still … having way too much fun doing what us Marines do best! Which you probably don't need to know about (not for girls)! Although I could SO do with a cold beer! Think this is the longest I've ever gone without one.

Just got my R'n'R date for a little leave and will be back around the first week in January so sadly will have to wait till then if you fancy a drink but more than up for a good drink and then teaching you a lesson on the dance floor!? Keep the msg's coming when you can. Will have to get you lots of drinks to make up for it.

Speak to you soon. x"

Although it was a constant battle of time difference, exercises, patrols and 'internet down time' we were able to message sporadically. I couldn't wait for his 'R and R' leave, because it would be the first time I would actually get to meet Paul on a one to one level. I was so nervous and ridiculously excited at the same time.

He finally arrived home on the 7th January 2008. Our first date was so nerve wracking. I didn't know where he was taking me or whether he would like me. We didn't really know each other. I put on my little black dress and straightened my hair, a full face of make up and I was ready to go. He picked me up in a taxi and as soon as I got inside he clapped his hand together and "Hiya Chick. Lovely to see you again!" As soon as I saw his smiling face, I knew that this guy was special! He didn't stop talking the whole way and this is the first memory that I wish I could remember forever.

The date went well. He took me to Nandos (I know first date in Nando's!) and then to the pub where we stayed until nearly four in the morning. I had to be up for work at eight, but I didn't care. I had just met the man of my dreams and the hangover was worth it.

For the next two weeks of his leave we were inseparable. I had a job interview for United Arab Emirates Airline which went well. We spent our first night together in a five star hotel overlooking Cardiff Marina. I didn't want him to go back and I knew I was falling for him. I knew what he was going back too. I knew all about the long distance relationship, the late night phone calls, the phone connection dropping off, the intermittent internet access, the down time on all communications, and worst of all, I knew about the fear of that dreaded knock at the door.

The night came when we had to say good bye. Paul dropped me home and he had dinner with my family and said good bye to me. I closed the door, walked into the living room where my Dad was sitting and cried. I didn't know why I was crying, as I knew it was going to happen, I knew he had to go back, but I also knew that I liked Paul a lot. Four months without seeing him seemed like a lifetime and the worry of potentially never seeing him again after the best two weeks of my life was unbearable. My parents are both ex- military and were very supportive. My Dad just hugged me and said "You really like him don't you?"

The following day I woke to hear my phone ringing – it was Paul, telling me he was just about to board his flight back to Afghan. He thanked me for an amazing two weeks and promised me that he would be safe. He finished the conversation with the words "I love you." I was shocked and stuttered "Urm Bye!" and put the phone down. I thought he had said it by mistake and it wasn't until I text him to clarify, that he said he more than liked me...in fact he loved me. I told him I loved him back.

Three weeks later I found out that I had got the job at United   Arab

Emirates, which meant moving to Dubai. I had no way of telling Paul except through Facebook messages. He was so pleased and couldn't wait to start this new adventure with me. He thought he would get cheap flights and holidays to Dubai, which never actually happened. But he was proud of his 'air hostess girlfriend'. I spent eight weeks doing my training in Dubai without hearing from Paul. I was extremely homesick and cried most nights. I couldn't call Paul, so I would call my best friend Melissa to reassure me every day. When Paul finally phoned I was close to passing my training. I was surprisingly strong on the phone to him; I wanted to show him that I was strong and having a great time. He didn't need to be worrying about me.

When Paul finally came home from Afghanistan we were able to have more of a structured long distant relationship. We could actually text and call each other which was amazing but we still had a time difference of four hours. Three weeks after he came home he arranged to fly out to Dubai and meet me. I was so excited that I arrived at Dubai airport before his flight had even left the U.K. I drank lots of coffee and walked around the airport for hours. When his flight finally arrived I noticed the taxi queue was starting to fill up, so I decided to join it and text him, so we weren't waiting for ages. I just wanted to get him to myself. I kept looking out for him but he surprised me, I turned around and he was behind me like a tall knight in shining armour. I was so excited I jumped on him and just squeezed him to death. It was the best two weeks holiday ever and then I got to fly back to the U.K with him for another two weeks. The moments we did get to share we so amazing and magical that it made the distance and hardship easier to bear. I worked for United Arab Emirates Airline for just under a year, and eventually left because the distance and homesickness took its toll. At the time my Dad was also taken ill thankfully he recovered, but it made it much harder being away from family. I was fed up missing birthdays and missing nights out with Paul and my friends; just missing him. I applied for the job before I met Paul and he gave me more of a reason to want to stay at home. Even later when my parents moved to Oxford to be with my Nan, Cardiff was always going to be my home, my friends and extended family were there and so was Paul. So, I decided I needed to be in Wales with Paul.

The biggest challenge of our relationship, and Paul's career, was when he applied for Special Forces. I knew he wanted to do it to improve our lives and the future for our children. But it was hard work. Our relationship was fine the whole time, we were a strong couple, but I knew whilst he was training that I had to be his rock. I had to tell him to keep going if he wanted to give up or when it got difficult. I had to change his mind set when he thought he wasn't good enough. I had to be the happy one and plan weekends when he was on leave to take his mind off the course. I was on the other end of the phone when he was afraid of never seeing me again before he jumped out of an aeroplane. I had to deal with his anger and pick him up when he failed the course. For three years he put his body through physical and emotional strain until he finally achieved a life's dream and passed. I was his rock during that time, but he was also mine. He was my hero for enduring all they put him through until he finally achieved his dream. In June 2012 Paul was passed into the Special Boat Service as a Royal Marine; the most elite fighting force in the world. It was the happiest day of his life.

During the time it took to pass his Special Forces course we talked of marriage, and like all couples, planned our future together. We decided we wanted to move in together and buy our own home. Paul was quiet and very much loved his home comforts and his family. He had a great work life balance and no matter what he had been through during the week he always left it at the door and made the most of his time with the family. He would never say a bad word about anyone, would never judge anyone. He was the sort of person who would give you his last penny, even if it meant he would go without. He had a close circle of friends both at home and at work and he always made time for them, making sure they were involved in anything he did.

Whilst we were looking for a house close to his family, his parents decided to sell their home to move in across the road with Paul's grandfather to care for him. So we had the perfect solution – we bought Pauls' family home.

On Wednesday October 3rd 2012, the day was like no other. The weather was awful; you always remember the weather. I was at work and everything was normal. I spoke about Paul a lot, and was showing people pictures, which wasn't unusual but looking back I wonder whether I spoke about him more than usual that day, as though I had some kind of sixth sense that something was wrong. I finished work at six and walked to my car. I hadn't heard from Paul all day which was strange, so I text him to let him know I was driving home and I would let him know when I got home safely, because of the weather. He always liked to keep me safe and was very protective, even when he wasn't physically with me. I got home about six forty and had arranged for my best friend Melissa to come to the house for dinner at seven. About ten past seven I heard a knock at the door and shouted for Melissa to come in. She didn't which was strange so I went to the door. There in front of me were two men in suits looking very smart. They asked for "Mrs Woodland?"

We had only owned the house for three months so I knew they were looking for Paul's Mum. I said "She isn't here at the minute, does she know you're coming?" They told me they were from Royal Marines Poole. I was completely confused and asked them over again where they were from, but I didn't understand why they were at my front door. So I went across the road to the fetch Pauls' Mum. As soon as I told her two men were at the door asking for her and were wearing suits, she knew. She just said to me "Oh No, Paul!"

We crossed over to my house and I was trying to reassure her saying, "No it's fine. It's probably to do with him passing his course and security check ups." As we walked down my drive she said to the men "Please, don't tell me it's bad news?"

"Unfortunately Mrs Woodland, it is. Paul was killed this morning in a boating accident in Barnstaple." They asked her to go inside the house and she was physically shaking, crying and screaming. I was in complete shock. I didn't cry and in fact I think I was in denial. I just kept saying over "No, he hasn't. Alicia don't believe him. I spoke to Paul last night and he was fine."

The next few hours were a blur. The welfare person turned up and I couldn't even talk to him. I didn't want him in my house. My parents were living in Oxford and I had to phone them and tell them. All I remember saying was "Mum, I need you more than I have ever needed you in my life. Paul has died. They are telling me Paul has died and I don't know what to do! Please get here!" Family and friends started to turn up offering support, crying and holding us. The next few days were horrendous. I felt numb. I didn't sleep for over forty eight hours and had to take sleeping tablets to help me rest. The military came every day and talked us through every step, financial details, funeral details. We learnt that Paul was on a boating exercise when his boat overturned. He was caught underneath and drowned. There were several attempts to resuscitate him and he tried to hang on with several small heartbeats, but his body finally shut down and he was declared dead at the hospital.

When Paul died the overwhelming support from friends and family helped me survive. When I couldn't cook a meal there was always one on the table. When I ran out of tissue, someone was always there with a box. When I ran out of vases to put flowers in, someone always went and found one. When I couldn't sleep, someone was ready to stay with me. The support from the local community even to this day is overwhelming. People I have never met before, support me in more ways than they could know.

The Royal Marine Wives and Girlfriends support network group on facebook has helped me to smile again, and given me opportunities I needed to help with my grief; given me advice and have been the best friend I lost. The bond between these girls is special and I will forever be thankful of their support. The saying 'you know who your friends are during tough times' is so true.

I know that Paul is still with me like a guardian Angel. I have had many signs that he is still looking out for me. I often receive white feathers which they say is a message from your guardian Angel. I find them in the most peculiar places and always when I am going through a stage of grief or loneliness. The first time I found one I was in my office checking emails and as I turned around to leave, on the floor in front of me was a huge white feather, and I just knew it was a sign from Paul. I felt he was with me that day. I love to collect them to keep him close to me and they sit in a beautiful glass jar on my mantle piece.

Another sign I think he sent me was about four months after he died.

The night Paul died his Dad told me I was meant to be a 'Woodland' and asked me to still change my name, even though we weren't married. Four months later, that was what I planned to do. I had asked Paul for a sign that he was happy with me changing my name and had nothing. I found it really hard being alone in our house so I was staying with his parents. I walked over to our house to check the mail. On the floor was a pink envelope – when I picked it up it was addressed to Mrs S Woodland. It was a card and cheque from Paul's extended family who I had actually never met. This was the sign I was waiting for and it gave me peace that Paul was happy I had changed my name.

I started fundraising in Paul's memory less than three months after he died; the main reason being that I never wanted people to forget him. I still don't. It scares me to think that all the hard work he did in his life will be a waste if no one remembers him. This is why everything I do is in his memory and I am determined to speak about him daily to make sure he is never forgotten. Since his death I have raised over £30,000 in his memory. The biggest thing I have achieved is climbing Mount Kilimanjaro. It was a huge challenge mentally and physically. I always told Paul I would climb it one day, and never for a second, thought that he would die and that I'd be climbing it in his memory. Thinking of Paul every step of the way helped me achieve a life's ambition.

Fundraising was something to channel my grief and it has given me a sense of belonging and purpose. It made me get up in the morning and has led me to meet people in the same position as myself. I now work full time for Forces Support Charity. I am their Community fundraiser and I manage a team of volunteers. It keeps me busy and I travel all over the UK meeting bereaved families, and like minded military supporters. It helps me come to terms with Paul's death as I have a new purpose now in life. I help others and I do it for Paul. It means I can talk about him daily and smile. I can help people with their grief because I understand and have lived through it, not just with the initial shock but also the long term sadness that never quite goes away. I initially did fundraising myself for the charity in my spare time, to directly honour Paul. Now working for the charity means that in my spare time I can concentrate on myself and moving my life forward with Paul by my side.

Ultimately Paul's strength, bravery and courage shine through me. I know he walks beside me and is proud of what I have achieved. I am strong, because he was so strong. I have learnt to remain positive and only see the positive in anything that happens now in life. I feel that although Paul has died, I don't have to give up on my life and that I have been given a second chance at it and happiness.

I am excited about the future. I am excited to inspire people, and give them hope in any aspect of life. Never struggle through life unhappy. Always smile; you never know who you will inspire.

Rollercoaster Ride

Erika, Royal Navy Wife

I tend to find myself describing our lifestyle as a rollercoaster ride and whilst there are always other things happening, I tend to put it mainly down to our military background. Unless you are in the forces yourself, I feel you can't really prepare yourself for marrying into the forces. I have heard it said so many times "You knew what you were letting yourself in for" but you really don't. When Alan is away, or our plans have to be changed, I still get angry and frustrated. You never learn to just live with it really.

My biggest achievement so far is my children. I was working in a high street chemist whilst studying my Health and Social Care when I met Alan, and I continued working once my maternity leave for our first child had finished. However, the nursery fees were taking the majority of my salary and having no local family to help when Alan was away we decided I would take a career break until the children go to school.

Although being a military family is hard and very worrying at times I personally think we are a stronger unit for experiencing this journey. I know I am a stronger individual and we appreciate each other's company rather than taking it for granted. Nevertheless that doesn't stop me sometimes resenting our civilian friends when they can enjoy family holidays that we can never seem to plan for. We have four children ranging from eight years to twenty-two months, and all they know is this lifestyle. As they are getting older, it is getting slightly easier on all of us. They understand it more now and the majority of their friends are from a forces background so that helps. When they were younger we had a calendar and a countdown chart in their bedroom which would help with deployments. We tried Skype once but unfortunately our oldest was very upset that he couldn't actually see his Dad. So, we decided to stick to emails and phone calls after that. It's all a learning process.

Last year I feel was our toughest battle. We celebrated the birth of our youngest son in January 2013 and Alan joined his new ship in the February. However, Alan became ill in the March and is still now undergoing medical investigations. Due to the amount of time he has been downgraded we are now facing the medical board in June to discuss discharge from the

Navy. Although I know that, whatever the outcome, we are going to be ok as a family unit, it still doesn't stop us worrying about changing our home and the children's school. We are currently just taking one day at a time and dealing with any problems that may come our way as a family.

"When My Daddy is away I feel a bit sad and a bit happy, so I just feel O.K."

Matthew, 5

79

"My Daddy has to fix and work on boats. I want to be a diver on a massive ship when I grow up."

Jason, 5

Abbie, 7

Suffering in Silence

Louise, Royal Marine Wife

The first time I met my Husband was on a typical Thursday night, on Poole Quay, I was stood in a bar called 'The Nelson' having a drink with friends when I saw this tall, bald headed man. After a few exchanged glances and smiles, I turned to my friend to say how nice he looked to which she replied, "I know him" and off she went to speak with him. After a while she returned and she had told him I liked him, I was a bit embarrassed, but also excited and enjoying my night out. That was it; we left the pub and went to a club. After a while I saw him again and he approached me. He was very sweet and lovely, we talked for a while but he said although he was flattered that I liked him, unfortunately he had a girlfriend! We said good bye and although I was disappointed, he had been honest, and it actually made me like him even more for his honesty.

After that we didn't have good timing with each other, and one of us was always in a relationship when we saw each other. It was nearly a whole year until we finally met both being single. We spent the night talking and he invited me back for a drink, we were joined by a friend and spent the night watching films. We agreed to meet again and we have been together ever since.

Two years into our relationship he got a draft to Plymouth. We weren't married so I assumed, and worried, that we wouldn't last much longer, but he surprised me and asked me to move with him. He brought a house for us near his base; I didn't know anything about the area which was a bad thing. The drive down the street was a shock as houses were boarded up and it didn't look great, but the house he had bought was nicer than the area, and soon became my safe haven. I was only there for four months when he went away for six months. This was to become my hardest time. I was so lonely, I started smoking again and drinking to get me through. My days would start with taking my dog out then I went to work. I only worked with men, who were all older than me so I rarely went out to socialise. I would come home and if it was dark I was scared to go back out. If I could, I would force myself to take the dog out again. That was me, for most of the time and was how I spent my day; only going out if I needed to. Looking back, I realise how depressed I was but I never asked for help. I didn't want to tell my mother how hard I found it. She was too far away to do anything and besides, she would only worry. I was ready to leave my partner and decided when he got back from his deployment that I would finish it. I couldn't do it when he was away. I knew he was under a lot of pressure whilst away so I didn't think it was fair to break up with him over letter or email. The time came closer and he was half way home when his ship was turned around. I sat and watched on T.V as they evacuated civilians from Lebanon, Beirut. Although I was proud of him, I was so upset I just cried. I wanted him home, and I wanted to go home and be with my family and friends.

It was two more months before he finally returned. I remember that day like yesterday, I saw him coming down the gangway of the Ship and everything in that one moment changed. My love for him wiped away the last eight months and I knew I couldn't leave him. How could I?

We went away on a holiday and it was there he asked me to marry him. I thought he was joking but after realising he was serious I said yes straight away. Our wedding day was such a great day! We were surrounded by friends and family.

Since then we moved back to Poole and now have two beautiful kids. Life has never been so good. I've never let myself get to the stage I was at, in Plymouth and I don't think I ever will. I've made a point of making friends and helping with camp life where I can.

The only advice I would give myself and anyone else is to be honest, and don't be afraid to ask for help. There are so many more groups online now, to join and use to meet people. Everyone has been or is in the same boat. Don't suffer in silence.

These men go away and come back into our lives and cause havoc.

Our kids are just learning that, and they don't like Daddy going. I'm sure he hates leaving although he doesn't show it; sometimes it's easier just to get on with things and not talk about how hard they are. We are honest with our kids and explain that he has to go, but, like he promised with me, he always brings them something back from wherever he has been. Even if it's a packet of love hearts. We also count down the sleeps until he's home, which they love, and it makes it easier for me to get them to sleep on my own.

My partner hasn't got long left to serve, so we have now started to talk about what he will do next. I'll be honest I'm more nervous than him. I have got used to this life and the different events we have throughout the year. I don't want to give that up yet;

I enjoy my weeks alone to watch and cook what I like, it makes me appreciate him so much more and I can't wait to see him. So, over the last thirteen years we have been up and down but we are now stronger than ever because of it.

"When he's [Dad's] away I feel I have to help Mummy more than ever because she usually struggles by herself with looking after me, my brother and our dog."

Taylor, 11

Precious Time

Loneliness. It haunts her; it dictates and fills her mind.
Again the words I'll "see you soon" cut a little more inside.
For she knows it's not a choice, but something that has to be.
No return dates given, more time apart the hurt he cannot see.
The weeks are long, the months will pass, the little one grows older.
A smile is shown so big and proud but weighs heavy upon her shoulders.
Time is precious, the little they have and impossible to share.
But he never understands the pain she feels when he's away and not there.
Still she smiles and sits in the back ground so he doesn't have to worry.
Friends and family all share the time, like it's all one massive hurry.
The day comes again to say those words and no precious time was saved.
For she sat watching everyone smile as her soul started to fade.
The time is important and precious and it slowly ticks away.
But she'll never stop hoping that the time will be hers, at least one day.

By Rebecca Louise Urrman. Royal Marine Wife.

"My Dad works in the Army, which I think is both good and bad."

Taylor, 11

My Story as a Royal Marine Wife
Elizabeth Eager

I have been with my Royal Marine eleven years of his thirteen year career, and I am always telling people about the untold bravery of the military wife. Our battles are often quietly won and we make many, many sacrifices to support our partners in the career they have chosen. It is important to remember that whilst we chose the man, we didn't choose the career for them or ourselves, yet its impact on our lives and the lives of those closest to our hearts – namely our children, is huge.

During our time together I have shared the dreaded fear of Afghanistan and the poor communication of a long ship deployment; and over the years I may have become blasé about our lifestyle. The wedding anniversaries that are missed pale into insignificance when you had to count yourself lucky he made it to the wedding at all. The birthdays spent alone are awful, but at least he was there to share the birth of our children – not all of my friends have been so lucky!

I met my husband just before he deployed to Iraq in 2003. When he told me he was in the Royal Marines - I had no idea what he was talking about! I had never heard of the Royal Marines, and I think I offended him a few times referring to his being in the Army. He soon put me straight! The only 'Wag's I knew of were footballer's wives and girlfriends – and that was a lifestyle I could see myself living, shopping, nightclubs, the occasional magazine cover, and a 'Hello!' deal to pay for your wedding. I was so immature and had literally no idea what I was about to let myself in for. I had just met a very hunky, fun and sexy guy that I instantly felt connected to. Although he didn't ask for my number on our first meeting, I wasn't about to be put off and wrote to him during his deployment in Iraq.

I suppose in some ways you could say waiting nearly six months for a first date, did give me some idea of what the lifestyle involved (lots of waiting!) But in other ways it didn't. I was young and naive and falling in love with somebody over old fashioned letters, blissfully unaware of the difference he would make to my life. It wasn't long after he came back from Iraq that we got engaged, and I started to really take notice of my life and the things I wanted from my future. Being with him was top of my list; the sacrifices that I would have to make to do it were so far down the bottom of the list that they were irrelevant. I always imagined that when I fell in love – it would be the man that would move Heaven and Earth to be with me, not the other way around. I had never imagined a life for myself outside my 'suburban bubble', surrounded by my friends and family. I hated my own company and would only ever go shopping with my Mum, or my sisters or my best friend. I honestly don't think I'd ever spent more than a few hours in my own company – there was always somebody on the end of the phone, or just a short bus ride away. I always thought I would be the centre of my future husband's universe. I couldn't comprehend the reality of sharing him with the military, of the promises he couldn't quite make because of work. Before I met him, I never knew how patient I was, or how brave. The realities of this lifestyle are harsh at times – and you can't comprehend what it will be like, how hard it will be, or how it will shape you as a person, until you've lived through it and come out the other side.

I grew up very quickly when we moved to a new city, a place I'd never been to before, on a Saturday, with six boxes, two suitcases and a blow up air bed, and then he left for a three week exercise on the Monday. I didn't drive, I didn't know how to cook (I still don't really!) I had no job, very little savings and no friends. It was my first taste of independence and homesickness, and it was a tough battle for me. I cried every day. But also, when he was home, it was a time of lots of fun and memories, and ultimately a time for me to grow up and become a stronger person. I never doubted that I still wanted to marry him and live this life. I just had to find a way to stop crying every day.

Eventually I got a job and we were able to save and 'crack on' with plans for our wedding day. That kept me focused and gave me something to look forward to. But even that the military had to make harder to endure, and he was deployed for six months prior to our wedding. Luckily I got the opportunity to fly out to Dubai and visit him which broke up the deployment nicely and gave me a nice pre – wedding tan.

But that holiday in itself was a huge challenge for me – I'd only ever been abroad twice. Once was an organised trip, where I turned up at the airport and flashed my passport, and the other was with my fiancé, which he had organised. I had no idea how to even start booking flights, hotel, transfers, insurance – but I did it! I flew to a country on the other side of the world, that didn't speak English, and I did it by myself!

Three months later and twelve days before our wedding, I was buying sun cream in a high street chemist when my husband-to-be phoned me. He sounded 'off' and I knew something was wrong immediately, but he refused to tell me what. He said he would call me back in an hour. I abandoned my shopping and went straight home to wait patiently for this call. There was no Wi-Fi in those days but as soon as I got in I started up my dial up internet and saw, eventually, that his ship had been delayed. He was four days from home and they were sending him back to the Middle East for a further eight weeks to rescue ex-pats from Lebanon.

Our wedding! I was beside myself!

I don't actually remember what I did for the next few hours, probably running through all the things that needed cancelling in my head. He finally phoned me back four or five agonisingly long hours later and told me they were flying him home for the wedding. He would be back with ten days to spare, but our wedding would be down about a dozen guests due to his ship mates still being deployed. So much for a Hello! Magazine cover - they probably couldn't have handled the drama!

It seems that every big life event we have is somehow punctuated with a big deployment. When we were expecting our first born, he was deployed to Afghanistan when I was just ten weeks pregnant and came back ten days before I gave birth. That was the toughest tour for me as he couldn't get R & R (two weeks rest and relaxation at home). He had to save it to be certain that he would get home early enough to see the birth of his son. But a nonstop, six month tour on the front line of Afghanistan took its toll on both him and me. I spent six months counting down until he came home, but when he got back we struggled as a couple. I had grown up and so had he; and we also had to learn about becoming parents for the first time. Whether we want them to or not, our experiences shape and change who we are. We loved each other more than anything in the world, and we were about to have a child together, but we had both changed and it took us a long time and a lot of effort to find each other again, and get back to the couple we were before he left. It's one of the things people never talk about – the adjustment and the change when they come home. It's also one of the areas that the military is sadly lacking in terms of support. Unless you are injured or diagnosed with PTSD[14], it is hard to find any

14. PTSD – Post Traumatic Stress Disorder

signposts of support, or any tips and tricks to help you and him re-adjust. You just have to fight through it, with equal amounts of understanding, communication, friendship, love and humour – there's always got to be humour involved when you're dealing with Bootneck's.

All of this aside, my biggest personal battle has come recently, trying to support my husband through some pretty serious health issues. He has always been the healthiest person I know – never even taking Paracetamol. There had been times when he was due to go away again, that I used to hope for an illness to delay his parting, nothing serious, but something that would mean he wouldn't have to leave me, but of course that never happened. He was as healthy as an Ox, and always left, on time, cheerfully for his next draft, exercise or deployment. So when he was finally due to spend an extended period of time in the UK, I was ecstatic. We'd just had our second child, and also had a two year old boy who had become painfully accustomed to his Dad being away all the time. This was going to be our time. We were going to get to spend quality time together as a family and we had lots of plans for holidays and fun days, and memory making.

When he was taken ill, all that changed. Yes he would be in the UK, but the fear of losing him still terrified me. We had never fought an enemy as unpredictable as the human body before. He had been diagnosed with a possible heart rhythm disorder and I watched him have CPR performed after going into cardiac arrest.

The fear was crippling. I was terrified of losing him again. It was the same fear that haunted me during Afghanistan, but this time I was also angry. I was so resentful that after all the time I had been supporting his career and waiting for "our time", and now it had been stolen from me and replaced with more fear. It was a difficult time for me, and I am ashamed to say I wasn't as supportive to him as I should have been. He was always my strength, my rock and my shelter. When he needed me to return the favour and be strong for him – well his boots were big ones to fill, and I wasn't as strong as I should have been for him.

Being in the Marines also means that your health has a huge knock-on effect to your career. He was, and possibly still will, face medical discharge. This terrified me. Our lives would change drastically if that was the case. We would have to buy a house as we currently live in military accommodation, and both our families live in an expensive part of the U.K How would we pay a mortgage?

I also found myself facing a kind of identity crisis. Being a military wife had defined so much of my life for such a long time – I didn't know what sort of wife I would be in a "normal" relationship. It has taken me a while to realise that my closest ally in all of this upheaval and fear is actually my husband himself. He shares the same fear, the same insecurities and worries. We have found the strength to face whatever changes and challenges our future may hold, together.

You have to marry for love, not because you want to change them or their career, but because you love them as they are. But in a forces relationship you have to be careful not to let the Love get forgotten because of the loneliness during deployments. We've been through many ups and downs, but we have always faced things together; as friends and lovers. That's what has got us through and kept us strong as a couple.

"Daddy is fighting enemies and baddies. He's a Royal Marine. When I grow up I want to be a Royal Marine and a footballer."

Matthew, 5

Saying Goodbye

Amy Wife of former Royal Marine

When I met James, he was already in the Marines and it was easy to get used to the lifestyle. To be honest, the most he was away with the Marines was for three weeks at a time. What we did struggle with was when James came out of the Marines; it was very hard for him to accommodate and get used to the life outside the Corps[15]. When he finally got a job locally he found it hard because the lads were nothing like his mates from the Marines. This had a massive impact on our family life and there were ugly times but we came out ok in the end.

We carried on with our lives as best we could when he first left the Marines. We moved from where James was based in Poole, back up North to where he is originally from, to be closer to his family as mine are abroad. Initially he was doing maritime security and I continued being a Mum, and looking after the house and our two daughters. When we first moved here, my time was awful. I found it very hard because I didn't have any friends of my own. I had left them all behind back in Poole, and I only ever got to see James's family. I felt very isolated; especially because he was away more now; sometimes for three months at a time, which was worse than in the Marines for me.

I started to notice that when James used to come back from his trips, he was angry a lot and never wanted to speak to me about it, just pushing me out. He always said he was fine, but you could tell he wasn't really. I specifically remember on one occasion when he came back, he was playing golf with his Dad on a Sunday. He left as usual, at 8 am and I wasn't expecting him back until at least 2 pm. But on that day he came home at eleven and said he was having a bad game, so he had to leave. This was not like him at all as he never gives up. He went straight to bed and didn't get up for the rest of the day! Even with my best efforts to try and get through to him. The next day was exactly the same..... I started to panic because he wasn't speaking to me or eating, and I was struggling with the girls who were both still so small. This was totally out of his character and a side to him I had never seen before.

---

15. Corps refers to The Royal Marine Corps.

I realised that I needed to get some help. So, I got his Dad to come and talk to him. His Dad is ex-military, so I figured he might be able to get through to him in a way that I couldn't. Even to this day I don't know what exactly was said, but I found out the reason he was feeling like he did; he felt he had no purpose anymore. He was struggling to adapt to day to day normal life, and he desperately missed his time in the Corps.

What I didn't realise is that for the last nine years his life was completely regimented. There was always someone telling him what to do, how to report, what to do about it, how to behave. Now he had no one to guide him, and I think he felt lost.

It took some time to come out of this and we're still adjusting now. He has a new job, and new colleagues, but they don't live up to the standards of his mates he had in the Marines; they all want an easy ride at work or look out for themselves and he sees them as disloyal.

I've learned to live with it and carry on. I think so has he, eventually. The girls help to keep us busy and make us appreciate the good times we have together as a family.

I think coming out of the Marines with no proper support has a big impact on the lads, married or not. The adjustment back into 'Civvie Street'[16] is a tough battle and one they almost have to do completely on their own. I class myself lucky because looking at the big picture it could've been worse, and at least we still have each other, and our beautiful daughters.

---

16. "Civvie street" is a military slang term referring to life as a civilian, outside of the military.

"We Facetime with Daddy or we call a lot. I feel sad when I can't see him."

Seth, 5.

A Love that Lasts.

Leanne, wife of former Royal Marine.

My husband Nick and I first met when we were just fifteen as we had a group of friends in common. I always fancied him but felt that he was out of my league; little did I know that four years later he would be the man to sweep me off my feet.

In 2003, Iraq happened and Nick was having leaving drinks with our mutual friends in the place where I worked. I gave him a hug and told him to stay safe and off he went. Over the next couple of months I would check the news regularly and I remember thinking how scary it must be for his family. Luckily he made it home safe and well, and we all met for drinks again to welcome home the very tanned hero. It was not long after this that our relationship started as it was clear to everyone that we were crazy about each other. I just knew we were meant for each other and didn't really think too much about how being with a Royal Marine would affect my life; that part of the relationship is just a happy blur of memories and young love.

Our first big trip came in January of 2004. It was an exercise to Norway; three and half months without him. I won't lie, I was basically a mess. I had a full time job, but took lots of overtime each week to try and keep busy. I was like a lost, miserable puppy. I wouldn't go out apart from work, and stayed home a lot! Back then he could only call on the landline and I would be so annoyed if I missed a call. It was from this point on that my sleep issues started, which still, to this day, I struggle with. He always laughs at me because when he is here at night, I cuddle into him and I'm out for the count, even if we are trying to watch a film. I just feel so relaxed with him next to me that I fall asleep in seconds. But when he's away I struggle, and sometimes I'm awake most of the night. Back during the Norway trip I would sit up and watch 'Friends' DVD's so now whenever he's away I find the only way I can fall asleep is by having Friends on in the background.

Just a year and a half after getting together we were married. Everyone thought we were rushing into it but we just knew it was right. We have now been married ten years and have been blessed with three wonderful children; two boys and a girl.

In 2006 we had our first baby Jaden; it was a wonderful new adventure for us. I was ill straight after the birth, and fell asleep but woke up to find Nick holding our baby that he had dressed himself. He was a natural Daddy and it felt amazing lying there looking at the two of them.

Nick had also starting training to go out to Afghanistan in the September, so he was busy for a few months but we managed to squeeze in our first family holiday aboard before he went; which was a nice memory to keep me going during the first tour. Before he left we recorded a video of Nick reading a story to Jaden. Every night of the tour Jaden and I watched it, just so he would still have a connection to his Daddy. I kept telling Nick that of course Jaden would still remember him, but I was secretly worried too; six months is a long time in a baby's life. The weeks and days leading up to saying goodbye were just awful. One minute you're making the most of the time you have left and enjoying it; the next you're snapping at each other for no reason. I'm not really sure how you stay strong through a tour but I think it just shows the strength and power of Love. You're strong because you have to be and because Love makes you strong. Having Jaden was a great distraction as he kept me very, very busy but he was also a massive reminder of the hole we had in our lives; of the fact that Nick wasn't here. He also hardly slept which was so tiring, especially when I went back to work the month after Nick left.

We were very lucky that during this first Afghan tour, Nick was deployed to Oman for a couple of months. I was very relieved to know he was safe during that time and we were also able to text each other which was amazing because it made me feel closer to him. But the luckiest part was that he would be based there over Christmas. So even though he couldn't come home, we were able to fly over for ten days. It was a long journey on my own with a nine month old but it was so worth it. Jaden wouldn't go near Nick for at least an hour, which hurt Nick as he's a very 'hands - on Dad'. But once Jaden warmed to him again, all was fine and he finally allowed Nick to be his Daddy again. It was a great experience to have a hot Christmas and also go somewhere I wouldn't have chosen to go on holiday. We had a lovely time. The only problem with going out there is that I had to go through the goodbye again, which never gets any easier; it was made worse by the flight home with a very lively baby and a packed plane.

A couple of times that stick in my mind from our Afghan tours is when I remember hearing a knock on the door one day and getting to the top of the stairs, looking at the door, I froze as I could see police uniforms. I

95

don't know how I managed to answer the door, expecting the worst; only to find it was completely unrelated to Afghan and not even for us. You are so on edge all the time. It's hard to not let things affect you. I emailed Nick straight away making sure he definitely knew exactly how much I loved him.

Coming back from the first Afghan tour Nick seemed to cope really well which was great and we soon got back to being a little family again. There was a welcome home family's day for the lads and their families at the base. But one thing which really annoyed me at the time is an officer gave a speech. He thanked the lads and the families, which was nice, and then he said "Enjoy your leave, and then we can start getting ready for the next Afghan" What a way to completely deflate the enjoyment of him coming home and to bring us back to earth!

In 2008 it was time for history to repeat itself. In the March I had our second son Tyler, whilst preparing ourselves for Afghan tour number two, starting in the September. It was lucky that Nick was home for Tyler's birth, as it was so quick that he was delivered in the ambulance on the way to hospital! So, again when Nick left, I had a six month old baby to keep me busy; only this time I also had a hectic, strong willed, two year old! Saying goodbye never gets easier, it never stops hurting and feeling like your heart is being ripped from your chest, no matter how many times you do it. In fact, I think saying goodbye actually gets harder the more you do it. The 'practice run' of the first tour only made me more concerned for his safety. It didn't help that our youngest Tyler, became poorly not long after Nick left; he had a chest infection that lasted seven weeks, then German measles. I was completely and utterly drained. I spent many nights sleeping downstairs on the sofa with two year old Jaden on a mattress on the floor, because he didn't want to be on his own, and Tyler in his pram, as he struggled to sleep in a cot. I remember night after night laying there, constantly, rocking his pram throughout the night. It was hard, really hard.

Now that Jaden was older, he understood more that Daddy was gone and he really wasn't dealing well with it and started getting migraines. We had made him a 'Daddy book' with lots of photos of Nick in it, but it's still hard for them to understand. He would refuse to speak to Nick on the phone the whole time he was gone; yet I would hear him in his room talking to Daddy in the book. He would also say goodnight to the moon as "Daddy could see the moon too".

After many weeks of being drained from lack of sleep and poorly   kids I remember the first, and one of the only times, that I cried on the phone to Nick. I always tried my hardest to stay positive on the phone as we only got a few minutes a week to talk. But this time I just didn't have the energy to hold it together and not cry. When our minutes ran out, I was so upset. About ten minutes later he phoned back, as he had brought some minutes off another lad. He said "Right Leanne, grab the boys and put them in the double pram".

I said "Why would I do that I want to stay in and hide?"

He said "I know, but you need those chocolate cookies that you love and a bottle of wine!"

I got the boys and put them in the pram, and out we went with Nick still on the phone. The shop was only a minutes' walk away so Nick stayed on the phone with me. When I got back and said Goodbye, I was crying but for a different reason; I was crying with a smile on my face, thinking I have the most amazing husband in the world who still supported me through the hard times.

During this tour Nick came home in January for R & R. He decided to surprise us by not telling us he was coming home that day. That evening, my phone was broken and I was at my parent's house with no way of knowing; but I had a funny feeling he was home so drove back to find him in the garden. I have never hugged him so tight. I cried and cried as he held me for ages, happy and sad tears all rolled into one; I guess they were three months worth of staying strong, tears. The ten days flew by and our youngest started walking the last day before Nick had to leave again, which was an amazing memory to share. The night that he was going back I couldn't face driving him so his Dad came to get him. I can honestly say that was the worst feeling I've ever had. We went up to bed to watch TV as he was leaving late that night, and we were both clinging on tight to each other knowing what was about to happen. Just before the point of leaving I couldn't help myself I asked him the un-thinkable question – would he definitely be coming home. He held me even tighter and told me he promised there was no way he wasn't coming home. There was a knock at the door and it was time for him to go. I stayed in bed so I didn't upset him even more. But when I heard the door close I just couldn't help it, I jumped out of bed and ran out after him. I needed one more cuddle, one more kiss, and one more time of feeling safe and to take in his smell one last time. Going back into the house I knew that I had to pull myself together for the boys. Not knowing how I was going to do it was hard but I'm just grateful he left at night, as it gave me the chance to sob into my pillow during the night and compose myself by morning for my gorgeous boys.

The scariest part of this Afghan tour came about three weeks before they were due home. I was working and at the end of my shift I noticed a couple of missed calls from a lovely friend, whose husband was also in Afghan with Nick. My heart sank. I sat in the car shaking as I listened to the message to find out her husband had been in some kind of an attack, and at that point we weren't sure how bad the situation was. I phoned her back and luckily she had managed to talk to her husband by then. Nick managed to get onto MSN messenger when I got home and he was in a bit of a state, as he felt it should have been him out there not his mate. I hated not being able to actually be there for him as I could tell how much it had bothered him. Thankfully, physically, our friend was fine.

You meet some amazingly strong men and women along the way of being a Royal Marine Wife and a tour can really bring you together. I have some amazing girl friends that I couldn't have got through the tours without; one of them I didn't even know before the first tour. I received a text from Nick after he'd left, saying "this is my mates wife's number she's recently moved to Plymouth and only had a baby two weeks ago please can you text her". In civilian world that may seem a strange text, but not in the military world; that was the start of a great friendship with our crazy, funny, Welsh friends. Another of the girls lived in the same street and we kept each other company and sent text morale boosts to lift out spirits and our kids have become great friends too. One of the girls has been around since my wedding and I'm so glad she has. She and her husband have been my rock over the years with lots of situations, and I'm proud to have her as my sons Godmother and to be Godmother to their gorgeous children. Another really close friend, is a girl that I actually started school with, but we hadn't seen each other for years and had grown apart; she happened to marry a Marine, which brought us back together again as it deepens your friendship when you understand the lifestyle. Every one of these friends including their husbands, hold a special place in my heart because although

Nick has left the Marines now and we don't see them often, they are still amazing friends.

A few months after the second Afghan tour was over, Nick got posted to the training team at Lympstone for a couple of years. I wasn't really keen on moving, but the draft meant that Nick would be home a lot more than he had been up until now. Leaving Plymouth was hard. Even though it was only an hour away, it didn't feel close enough to my family who had always been a massive part of the boy's life. They were used to seeing them almost daily. But when we got there, I fell in love with the place. I got to our new home and I couldn't believe my luck as the house was massive and it was beautiful. The boys used to love it when Nick would take them onto the camp with him. It gave them more of a bond with him, which was great, as he had missed out on over a year of our oldest sons life. We spent so many family weekends together mainly at the beach. Things were going great but we knew Nick was due to be posted again soon and we knew it would mean joining the next Afghan tour. I wasn't sure if I could do it again, and to my surprise he didn't want to either. Nick loved the Marines; he really did, and was often called "Pussers Nick" amongst our Marine friends because he loved it so much. I was in shock when he told me he wanted to leave, but we sat and talked it through that night. He talked about doing maritime security as his new job, which I had never heard of. I wanted to be really sure he wanted to leave. I didn't want him to leave just because he thought it was what I wanted. But he was adamant, and had made up his mind. I couldn't believe that in a year, he would be out.

Leaving that house and Lympstone was awful. I cried so much, because that house was where I felt we properly became a family; it felt like our home. The two Afghan tours had taken over us being a "normal" family. In this house, in this village we were happy. Plymouth still felt like home as we had grown up there, but Lympstone had my heart. The two and half years of our life as a "normal" family in Lympstone, feels like an amazing dream that somehow didn't actually happen.

The last month that Nick was in the Marines was a stressful time. Although he had been taken on by two companies for his new job it was 'as and when' work so we were worried how long it would be before he got work or whether he would even get anything. Nick was on edge for weeks and it was a tense time of worrying whether it would work out, and if we had made the right decision. It was horrible.

The last three years have been hard with Nick finding his new job path and I found it difficult with letting go of our youngest son who has started school, especially knowing seven months of the year Nick will be away! How would I fill my days? Although I had always worked, it was now part time around the boys and I really wanted to have more children. Over the years Nick and I have suffered eight miscarriages or 'Angel' babies as we called them. It was devastating. Every time it happened was a new heartbreak and Nick didn't want to see me go through that again. We even considered adopting. However, shortly after him being home I woke up one morning in a lot of pain. Nick took me to the Drs and I got sent straight to hospital with suspected ectopic pregnancy. I had bloods and was booked for a scan where they found out that it wasn't an ectopic, but a healthy pregnancy. We were shocked but knew there was no point getting excited; we had been here before and this pain surely meant only one thing. We had to wait a few weeks for another scan to see what was going to happen but we had already got it in our heads that it would just be confirming what we already knew. Another 'Angel' baby. At the scan we found out there was still a heart beat! We couldn't believe it. Nick had to go back to work. But when I was sixteen weeks I booked a private gender scan. At this point Nick was away for four months and we hardly had contact. I was able to email him once a day but no photos. After the scan I sent him an email with just the words "ITS A GIRL!!!!!!!!!!!!!!!!!!"

The four months of him away were hard and the boys really struggled too, so Nick took until Christmas off, a choice he wouldn't have had whilst still in the Marines. He was around for the birth of our little girl. We had a home birth which was amazing, and because she had two knots in her cord, they said she could have been lost at anytime in the pregnancy; but she was a strong baby and the boys have adored their sister since the moment they came in that morning to find her in bed with us. Our family is now complete and she came into our life when we needed her most

There are so many emotional points sharing your life with a Marine. Sometimes when it's hard, you wonder why you bother, but I wouldn't have it any other way. It has made me strong, even though sometimes I feel I'm not, and it has given me experiences, memories and friends I would never have made. It's made me the person, the Mum and the wife I am now. If I had known the amount of times I would have sobbed, and the heartache experienced over our twelve years together; I would still not have ran the other way. I have a husband who adores me and is a great father and between the tough, horrible times I have the most amazing memories. Living this life makes you really make the most of the time you have together and I am proud to say I married a Marine.

Jaden, 8

When I was little I would say good night to the moon, because my Daddy could see it too."

Jaden, 8.

Warrior Wives

Epilogue

When I started this project, I had no idea how precious it would become; how much it would mean to me, and to the girls sharing their stories. Every one of the ladies who submitted a story said that in some way writing it down helped them. It helped them to realise their strength, or helped them to let go of the resentment they had been feeling. It helped them to heal and appreciate their value. Every one of the stories submitted moved me to tears, or made me smile in sweet recognition of the crazy things we do for Love. It is the Love that keeps us strong, when times are hard and the phone calls are infrequent, the kids are hyperactive, and the dog is sick, and the car is broken... It is the memory of that Love which sees us through.

To the ladies who shared their stories with me and opened their hearts; I thank you from the bottom of mine.

To other service Wives, Girlfriends or Partners who choose not to tell their tale – I thank you too. All of the Wives or Lovers who have lived this life before me, and all of the ones yet to do it: You won't often hear it from your Husband's/Partners, or from the mysterious 'hierarchy' that controls so much of our lives, but from me to you: Thank you for all you do. In my darkest, loneliest hours I knew deep in my soul that I wasn't really alone. I knew there were others who had been here before me, often with less technology and harder circumstances, and that knowledge gave me strength.

To the Husbands and Lovers that we wait for; it's harder than you know to be apart from you. When we're exhausted, from the pressure of staying strong, remember us in our happier moments, and know that we wouldn't change it for the world. And it goes without saying, stay safe wherever you are.

I hope you can see from these pages that we are just average families living an un-average lifestyle. We are not shielded from any of life's hardship; we have our financial struggles, relationship struggles, health worries and everyday heartbreaks too.

This book was not written to ask for sympathy or understanding, we don't expect you to understand or sympathise. It is not our intention to share with you all our hardships, but to relay some of the joy and pride we experience in our children and our partners, and in ourselves. Contrary to popular belief – we didn't know exactly what we were letting ourselves in for, and the ones who did, were reluctant to live this lifestyle. We still don't know what challenges lay ahead, we just live our lives in the best way we can with the circumstances we are given.

What we want is a voice, a chance to tell our tales and to share our experience; for our children to recognise a different kind of bravery; to leave our legacy of love.

Or perhaps we just want to be bought a beer once in a while...

Helpful Resources

Being part of a service family can bring its own unique set of challenges and obstacles. I have been living this life for over eleven years and only recently found out some of the support that is available. The support and resources are something that is, thankfully growing.

I thought it would be useful to share some of the information here, so if you are struggling, or know someone who is, you can perhaps offer them some guidance with this book. Although please understand that this is not an exhaustive list, but tools which I personally have found useful; and whilst it is correct at the time of going to print, things do often change and there are many other support groups, charities and organisations available, too many to feature completely here. For more information on these, contact your local Hive and Service Welfare link who will be able to signpost the best option for you and your family.

The Royal Navy and Royal Marines Childrens Fund

The RNRMCF was originally started as an orphanage over 100 years ago. It is the only charity dedicated to supporting children whose parents work, or have worked, for the Naval Service. It has grown immensely and with the long conflict in Afghanistan and the continued long deployments within the Navy, it is now needed more than ever. Around 80% of its beneficiaries have parents that are still serving. In the last year alone, The Royal Navy and Royal Marines Children's Fund has supported over 1,500 children, but with over 40,000 servicemen currently in the Naval Service, it is keen to ensure that Naval families know where to find them. Consideration of every circumstance is given sympathetic attention by people who understand the difficulties of service and seafaring life. They can provide support in a number of ways:

- support families at home when partners are away, at sea or in an area of conflict
- provide at-home support in times of crisis
- assist with childcare when a parent is unable to cope
- help children who have suffered bereavement
- help children who are suffering family break-down or parental divorce
- provide special family days out in times of grief or distress
- help families where there has been an injury or illness
- assist families with travel expenses so that they can travel to be together, or

to support children in hospital
- help educate children who are constantly 'on the move' or who have special needs
- provide specialist equipment for children with disabilities

Contact them via their website: http://rnrmchildrensfund.org.uk

RN & RM Children's Fund
311 Twyford Avenue
Portsmouth
PO2 8RN
E: rnchildren@btconnect.com
T: 02392 639534
F: 02392 677574

Social media can often be seen in a negative light, but for people who feel isolated, are living away from home, or because their immediate friends and family don't understand the situation they are living in; it can be vital. It can be a way to connect with others who are going through, or have previously gone through what you are experiencing. I wish I had the use of Facebook when I faced my first (and second, and third) deployment.

The Royal Marine Wives and Girlfriends Support Network

The Royal Marine Wives and Girlfriends Network initially launched a charity calendar in 2012, and set up a support network following on from this. The support network is for wives of serving or former Royal Marines and now has over 500 members. It is a place where its members share everything from job opportunities and fundraising to childcare tips and deployment advice or issues. The committee members and admin work hard to make sure that all posts are secure and do not give away any security details, and new members are vetted; because of this it is the only Facebook group that is supported and endorsed by the Royal Marines Charitable Trust Fund.

If you would like to join the network find them on facebook and message one of the committee members https://www.facebook.com/pages/Royal-Marine-WAGs-Calendar-2012 or email: rmwagscalendar@gmail.com

There are similar groups run for Wives of the Royal Navy and UK Forces Wags.

StoryBook Waves

Storybook Waves helps members of the Royal Navy and Royal Marines maintain the link with their children by recording a bedtime story for them to listen to when a parent is serving away from home.

The Royal Navy and Royal Marines deploy more frequently than personnel in the other services. Leaving loved ones behind when serving overseas or on board ship is a feature of life in "the most separated service." These separations can be especially difficult for children. Storybook Waves exists to help maintain the link between parent and child, no matter how far apart they may be.

Storybook Waves provides facilities for anyone serving away from home to record a bedtime story for their child. Once recorded, trained volunteer editors add a soundtrack and create a personalised CD for each child so that he or she can listen to a parent's voice whenever they want

For further information contact the project coordinator on 03003020183, email info@storybookwaves.org or go to the Storybook Waves website http://www.aggies.org.uk/storybook-waves-2

Service Pupil Premium

It is useful to know that all service children who attend school in the U.K are entitled to the Service Pupil Premium. It is a small amount of funding that is awarded to your child's school for them to spend in a way they feel would best support your child. Some larger service schools such as Goosewell Primary School who contributed to this book, pool their money to pay for a specialised support worker to support service children and act as a liaison for parents, or to run 'keep in touch' clubs; some schools prefer to use it to fund extra hours for Teaching Assistants to help pupils who may have gaps in their education due to moving; others prefer to use it to offer pastoral care during times of deployment. Different children have different needs that vary considerably. The Service Pupil Premium can be claimed by the school for up to five years after the serving person has left. It is important to make sure your child's school is aware that they can claim this funding, and although you are not able to dictate how it is spent, you know it will be benefitting your child.

https://www.gov.uk/government/publications/pupil-premium-grant

HMS HEROES

HMS HEROES started in Plymouth as an initiative to offer a peer support group for other service children. It is a tri-service group, meaning that it caters for all branches of the Armed Forces and has proven incredibly popular for Service and Veterans children and families. It is now offered in schools across the country and even abroad, with over 8000 members.

The children who are part of HMS Heroes join up at meetings to raise concerns, talk about worries and create fantastic projects.

The name HMS HEROES comes from the fact that even in your own home you can be a Hero. Whether supporting the parent left behind, caring for your brothers and sisters and being brave when your parent or family member is in a dangerous place. 'We are all heroes,' noted one ten year-old and it became the name.

The group is "a safe place to talk because you know your friends will understand how you feel because they feel the same". Many Heroes experience the trauma brought about by the cycle of service deployment and they value support that does not make them feel 'different'. At a recent meeting, some older Heroes reported the difficulty of studying war and conflict, because the lessons can trigger intense emotions. "I just have to get out of the room," said one girl, "my teacher wouldn't understand." Issues they talk through include their feelings related to the cycle of deployment and the death of a parent in Afghanistan.

Children need to feel included, and connected, but they don't have the coffee mornings or facebook groups that the adults are offered. HMS Heroes fills that gap.

Huggable Heroes

For younger children that may be suffering from separation anxiety or miss Daddy/Mummy there is Huggable Heroes. Huggable Heroes are designed to 'reinforce the bond between parent and child while Mummy or Daddy is working away and reduce the Separation Anxiety in our Brave Children.' It is a business idea set up by a Royal Marine wife and mother whose young children were struggling with their Dad's absence. She made them a cuddly doll with Daddy's photo on it for them to cuddle. Seeing how it benefitted them and reinforced the bond they had with Daddy she has now gone on to turn the great idea into a business.

Jo-Anne says "Huggable Heroes help enormously. Our Huggable Hero goes everywhere with us so he doesn't miss a thing. He was with Charlotte on her first day at Pre School and enjoys swimming and Gymnastic classes. Henry enjoys cuddles and play fighting with his Hero. Once I realised how much Huggable Heroes could help children with a parent working away I decided to offer them to all children, not just military. We have now helped children in hospital and autistic children. It is fantastic, and I hope that Huggable Heroes will help more children in all different walks of life. We also make Huggable Heroes of Children for Mummy or Daddy to take away with them for the very important cuddles."

www.facebook.com/HuggableHeroes @LottieLoveHenry on Twitter (Website coming soon www.HuggableHeroes.co.uk) email LottieLovesHenry@aol.com

ROYAL MARINES ASSOCIATION

The Royal Marines Association

The Royal Marines Association (RMA) exists to support serving and veteran Royal Marines and their families through every aspect of life, assisting in times of need, and offering practical support during the transition to civilian life. It maintains and promotes esprit de corps and comradeship amongst all Royal Marines and their families, past and present. The RMA is established in Branches all over the country and overseas to keep members in touch with one another. They are an integral part of the Corps Family.

The main purpose of the RMA is to support the Corps Family, including the Royal Marines Reserve and the Royal Marines Band Service. We raise funds for veterans and their families. The aim is to provide support to any member of the Corps Family when asked.

If you or your spouse is currently serving in The Royal Marines, The RMA exists to support you. Membership is inexpensive and is extended to Serving Royal Marines and their spouses, Retired Royal Marine's, Royal Marine Band, Royal Marine Reserve, and any member of a serving/retired Royal Marine's direct family (i.e Mum, Dad, Wife, Girlfriend, Sister, Brother)

And also any member of the Armed Forces that have served directly under the strength of an Royal Marine Unit.

Contact Details:
CEO - Mike Ellis:
mike@rma.org.uk

Operation Manager - Richie Puttock:
richie@rma.org.uk

Welfare & Opertions Assistant - Mark Ormrod:
mark@rma.org.uk

Membership - Chris Inkpen
chris@rma.org.uk

Welfare - Wendy Sheen
wendy@rma.org.uk
Find us on Facebook RMA or Twitter: @RMA1664

Other Resources:

Royal Marines Charitable Trust Fund http://www.rmctf.org.uk (023 9254 7201)
Naval Families Federation http://www.nff.org.uk/ (023 9265 4374)
Go Commando http://www.gocommando.org.uk/ (01963 31683)
Military Families Support Group www.mfsg.org.uk
Help for Heroes www.helpforheroes.org.uk
Combat Stress www.combatstress.org.uk (24 hour helpline 0800 138 1619)
The Royal British Legion www.britishlegion.org.uk Legionline 08547 725 725
My Daddy is a Soldier Adventures www.mydaddyisasoldieradventures.org
Forces Support http://www.forcessupport.org.uk/

Acknowledgements.

This book would not have been possible without the input of influence of so many people. First and foremost I need to thank the ladies who shared their stories; my 'Band of Wives' Group and The Royal Marine Wives and Girlfriends Support Network; without them this book would have forever remained an idea. Adele Towsey – your group is what started this! Before then I didn't realise my own strength and resilience. Your work may have felt undervalued at times, but I promise you for the people that needed it; it mattered.

I need to thank Monique Bateman at The Royal Navy and Royal Marines Children's Fund; her tireless optimism, and continued support whilst giving me creative freedom to do what I envisioned were driving factors in getting me to finish.

I would like to thank Heather Ogburn for her input regarding HMS Heroes and the Service Pupil Premium and her continued efforts to support Service children in State Schools. You do an amazing and much needed job. Also Jo Penks and Goosewell Primary School for their incredible and heartfelt support; not only for this book, but the support they offer to the military children they care for in the school. It is inspiring and comforting to see. I wish all military children could benefit from your level of understanding and care.

I also need to thank Amanda Prowse for her much needed inspiration, advice and support and Shani Struthers for not dismissing me and offering advice above and beyond what I could have hoped for.

Thank you also to Tim Mitchell at Tim Mitchell Design for his amazing efforts in getting this project into print and available – all for the price of a 'few wets'! Which I still owe you...

To Grant, Jane and Amy for their proof reading and encouragement – You are Stars! Payment coming your way in the form of beer or wine.

To Claudia, my beautiful artist, who put up with me having no real 'vision' and the occasional panic over how the book should look. Thank you for your time and you talent.

Last but, by no means least, thank you to my husband Al; my "Truth Teller"; your honesty, integrity, and constant encouragement has been second to none. I hope I can make you half as proud as you continue to make me.

"Elizabeth Eager's 'Warrior Wives' has captured the honesty and grit of twenty four remarkable women. These stories really highlight the highs and lows of life in the Naval Service from the families' perspective. The RN & RM Children's Fund is proud to play its part in supporting the children in times of need and crisis."

Monique Bateman,
Director of The Royal Navy and Royal Marines Children's Fund

"This is such an incredible project that I am delighted to support. It's wonderful to see military wives getting the voice they deserve. Buy the book and support these brilliant women who have been through their own battles and can now share their gripping, remarkable stories."

Amanda Prowse,
Author and military wife

"Read this book and understand military service from a different point of view. Prepare to laugh, prepare to cry but above all prepare to be moved, inspired and uplifted"

Chris Terrill

Printed in Great Britain
by Amazon